# Garden Design

# Garden Design

teNeues

Editor in chief: Paco Asensio

Editorial coordination: Haike Falkenberg, Cynthia Reschke

Project coordination and texts: Patricia Pérez Rumpler

Art director: Mireia Casanovas Soley

Layout: Gisela Legares Gili

Copy-editing: Francesc Bombí-Vilaseca

German translation: Bettina Beck

French translation: Michel Ficerai

English translation: Matthew Clarke

Published by teNeues
Publishing Group

teNeues Publishing Company
16 West 22nd Street, New York, NY 10010, US
Tel.: 001-212-627-9090, Fax: 001-212-627-9511

teNeues Book Division
Kaistraße 18
40221 Düsseldorf, Germany
Tel.: 0049-(0)211-994597-0, Fax: 0049-(0)211-994597-40

teNeues Publishing UK Ltd.
P.O. Box 402
West Byfleet
KT14 7ZF, Great Britain
Tel.: 0044-1932-403509, Fax: 0044-1932-403514

www.teneues.com

ISBN: 3-8238-4524-1

Editorial project: © 2002 **LOFT** Publications

Via Laietana 32, 4° Of. 92
08003 Barcelona, Spain
Tel.: 0034 932 688 088
Fax: 0034 932 687 073

e-mail: loft@loftpublications.com
www.loftpublications.com

Printed by: Anman Gràfiques del Vallès. Spain
July 2003

Bibliographic information published by Die
Deutsche Bibliothek. Die Deutsche Bibliothek lists
this publication in the Deutsche
Nationalbibliografie; detailed bibliographic data is
available in the Internet at http://dnb.ddb.de

Marianne Boesky Garden by Paula Hayes
Photo © John Peden

Previous page:
Van Egeraat Garden by Adriaan Geuze
Photo © Jerden Musch / West 8

# Introduction

The functions of the gardens presented in this book are not, generally speaking, any different from those of other gardens throughout history. They can be classified as gardens for recreation and relaxation (locus amoenus, hortus ludi), for representative functions, for open-air gallery-style display or as purely contemplative gardens (hortus contemplationis). Furthermore, these spaces can also be classified, according to their use, as private or public gardens, or as hybrids between the two. Although a garden can be imbued with varying degrees of significance, it never ceases to provide its users with the illusion of a domain that has been made to measure, of a place, like Paradise, whose existence is free from peril. The myth of the Garden of Eden still forms part of the cultural legacy of Muslims, Christians and Jews alike, and they therefore still influence our attitudes and feelings; they also provide clear evidence of the undoubted fascination that plants, and gardening in general, have exerted over human beings since time immemorial. Gardens have always existed and they always will, from the beginning to the end of our journey through life. However, this book does not seek to explore these timeless aspects but rather aims to provide a showcase for examples of alternative, unconventional ideas and reinterpretations of the traditional garden.

The modernity of the various projects on display here lies not only in the use of new materials and construction techniques but also, above all, in a shared common denominator: they are all small gardens in urban settings. If we accept the hypothesis that within ten years almost half of the inhabitants of the Earth will live in cities, then it is clear that the contemporary urban garden is something that robs space from the urban fabric, while also using it as a support and taking over its inner spaces. The following pages offer some striking proposals: gardens that climb up facades or nestle on rooftops, others that occupy the gaps between adjacent properties, or between a facade and a road. These examples are proof that gardens are now, more than ever, refuges that provide compensation for the frenzied dynamism of city life, spaces for winding down and enjoying peace and quiet within the hubbub of a metropolis.

The urban setting imposes a series of evident but complex limitations, but small, personal interventions often find subtle ways of overcoming them. Gardens may be minimal patches of land with an architectural layout, but they work like acupuncture points in the city: their benefits extend far beyond those of an isolated setting. This interstitial tendency turns these gardens into microcosms that help improve the quality of life of city dwellers. The gardens here are generally modest ones that are difficult to make work and are characterized by what they lack: a lack of space, a lack of fertile soil, a lack of time or a lack of light. All this is reflected in the strong presence of their boundaries, in hard materials confronting vegetal elements. However, far from being examples of failed intentions, they are veri-

table displays of ingenuity in situations marked by a lack of resources. In popular parlance, they are places in which people have tried to make a virtue out of necessity and have created gardens where there was practically no room for them.

The gardens presented in this book are far from being a privilege only available to an elite with plenty of money or land; instead, they represent widely accessible opportunities to recreate natural processes, even though these processes are often reduced to the bare minimum or are only discernible through symbolic allusions. Such is the case of ephemeral gardens—projects for gardens in which the concept of durability is of no importance, gardens that occupy a spot for a short period in order to attract attention to its special charac-

teristics or add a new twist to it. This tendency ultimately leads to the minimum expression of the garden in today's world: the flowerpot, typical of windowsills and balconies.

The strategies used by designers all over the world provide examples of the practical resources available to us and teach us that even this traditional recipient can become an evocative image of a "pocket garden" that even the most nomadic lifestyle can incorporate into the environment of asphalt and concrete that most of us share in our everyday lives.

Garden of Pershing Hall by Andrée Putman
Photo © Mihail Moldoveanu

D ie Funktionen der im vorliegenden Buch vorgestellten Gärten unterscheiden sich nicht von denen, die der Garten im Lauf der Geschichte immer innehatte. Man kann Gärten verschiedenen Gruppen zuordnen, je nachdem, ob sie der Erholung und Zerstreuung dienen (locus amoenus, hortus ludi), repräsentative Funktionen haben, als Ausstellungsräume unter freiem Himmel angelegt sind oder rein kontemplativen Zwecken dienen (hortus contemplationis). Darüber hinaus können diese Räume – je nach Nutzung – in private und öffentliche Gärten oder eine zwischen diesen beiden Polen liegende Mischform eingestuft werden. Einem Garten kann mehr oder weniger Bedeutung beigemessen werden, aber stets ist er doch ein Ort, der seinen Benutzern den Eindruck eines Reiches im übertragenen Sinne gibt, an dem sie sich – wie im Paradies – in ihrer Existenz nicht bedroht fühlen. Die Legende des Garten Edens ist immer noch Teil des kulturellen Erbes und bestimmend für Handlungen und Gefühle in der Gegenwart – für Muslime, Juden und Christen gleichermaßen. Ebenso sind Gärten zweifellos Ausdruck des Interesses, das der Mensch Pflanzen und Gartenbau im Allgemeinen stets entgegengebracht hat. Der Garten ist immer da gewesen und wird es auch weiterhin sein, von Anbeginn bis zum Ende aller Vorgänge. Es ist das Anliegen des vorliegenden Buches, neben dieser Zeitlosigkeit alternative Beispiele in den Vordergrund zu rücken, weniger konventionelle Register oder Neuinterpretationen des traditionellen Gartens.

Der zeitgenössische Charakter der verschiedenen hier vorgestellten Projekte beruht nicht nur auf der Verwendung neuer Materialien und Bautechniken, sondern vor allem auf einer Gemeinsamkeit: es handelt sich in allen Fällen um kleine Gärten in urbaner Umgebung.

Ausgehend von der Hypothese, dass in zehn Jahren die Hälfte der Erdbewohner in Städten leben wird, kann man die Behauptung aufstellen, dass der zeitgenössische urbane Garten dem dichten Bebauungsgeflecht Raum entzieht, es als Untergrund benutzt und seine Innenräume erobert. Unter den Lösungen auf den folgenden Seiten werden einzigartige Beispiele vorgestellt, wie an Fassaden hochkletternde Gärten, solche, die auf Dächern nisten oder die, welche die Räume zwischen Brandmauern und zwischen Fassade und Fahrbahn besetzen. Anhand dieser Beispiele wird deutlich, dass der Garten heute mehr denn je ein Ort des Ausgleichs innerhalb der hektischen urbanen Dynamik ist. Er wird zu einem Raum der Verlangsamung, des zur Ruhe Kommens und der Stille im Tosen der Großstadt.

Die urbane Umgebung schafft eine Reihe von klaren und komplexen Bestimmungsgrößen und oftmals sind es gerade die kleinen individuellen Eingriffe, die dazu beitragen sie auf kluge und subtile Art zu bewältigen. Es handelt sich meist um kleinstmögliche Bestandteile der Landschaft mit architektonischer Dimension, die in der Stadt wie Akupunkturnadeln wirken und deren Vorteile diejenigen eines isolierten Gartens überwiegen. Ihr Dasein in Zwischenräumen lässt sie zu Mikrokosmen werden, die dazu beitragen, die Lebensqualität

der Stadtbewohner zu heben. Im Allgemeinen sind es diskrete, nicht einfach zu realisierende Gärten, die sich allesamt durch einen „Mangel" auszeichnen: Mangel an Raum, an fruchtbarem Boden, an Zeit oder an Licht. All dies schlägt sich in einer starken Spürbarkeit ihrer Grenzen nieder und in einem Übergewicht harter Materialien gegenüber der pflanzlichen Komponente. Trotzdem sind sie keineswegs Beispiele fehlgeschlagener Bemühungen, sondern aussagekräftige Beweise für umgesetzte Erfindungskraft in Zeiten mangelnder Ressourcen. Es sind also, kurz gesagt, Orte, an denen aus der Not eine Tugend gemacht wurde und Gärten an Orten geschaffen wurden, die eigentlich keinen Platz für sie bieten.

Der Garten, so wie er im vorliegenden Buch dargestellt wird, ist bei weitem kein Privileg, das ausschließlich begüterten Gesellschaftsschichten oder Eigentümern größerer Grundstücke vorbehalten ist. Ganz im Gegenteil, er wird zu einer allen zugänglichen Möglichkeit, Prozesse der Natur nachzuempfinden. Um dies zu erreichen, werden die Gärten oftmals auf ein Minimum reduziert oder als solche nur symbolisch angedeutet. Dies ist der Fall bei temporären Gärten, bei denen dem Argument der Dauerhaftigkeit keinerlei Bedeutung zukommt. Es handelt sich generell um Garteninstallationen die nur kurzfristig Orte besetzen, um den Blick für die Eigenart des Ortens zu öffnen, oder um neue Erfahrungen hinzuzufügen. Auf diese Weise könnte man bis zur Minimalverwirklichung des Gartens von Heute gelangen, nämlich dem Blumentopf, wie er auf Fensterbänken und Balkonen zu finden ist.

Die von den Designern auf der ganzen Welt verfolgten Strategien zeigen ganz deutlich die praktischen Mittel, die uns dieser Aufgabe näher bringen und führen uns vor, dass sogar ein klassischer Behälter zum reizvollen Abbild des „Gartens in der Tasche", des „pocketgarden", werden kann. Gärten, die sogar bei der unstetesten Lebensweise ihren Platz in jenem alltäglichen Umfeld aus Asphalt und Beton finden, das die meisten von uns umgibt.

Taylor Cullity Residence Garden by Taylor Cullity Lethlean
Photo © Edward James / Ben Wrigley

L a fonction remplie par les jardins présentés dans cet ouvrage ne diffère aucunement de celle exercée par le jardin au cours de l'histoire. Les jardins peuvent être classifiés entre les lieux de loisirs et de détente (locus amoenus, hortus ludi), ceux assumant des fonctions de représentativité, les jardins-salles d'exposition à l'air libre ou ceux essentiellement contemplatifs (hortus contemplationis). D'autre part, selon les usagers, ces espaces se répartissent entre jardins privés, publics ou hybrides, entre ces deux extrêmes. Bien qu'un jardin puisse être plus ou moins chargé de sens, il ne cesse cependant jamais d'être un espace offrant à ses habitants l'illusion d'un domaine figuré où, comme au ciel, son existence semble libre de toute menace. La légende du jardin d'Éden, pour les musulmans comme pour les chrétiens et les juifs, fait encore partie de notre legs culturel, étant responsable d'attitudes et de sentiments présents. Ainsi, les jardins sont un signal incontestable de l'intérêt incessant de l'homme envers les plantes et le jardinage en général. Le jardin a été, est et sera toujours là, début et fin de tous les processus. Pour autant, en marge de cette intemporalité, cet ouvrage a choisi de mettre en exergue des exemples de registres alternatifs, peu conventionnels, ou de nouvelles interprétations du jardin traditionnel.

La contemporanéité des diverses propositions exposées naît non seulement de l'emploi de nouveaux matériaux et techniques de construction, mais aussi et surtout d'un dénominateur commun unique : tous sont des petits jardins dans un cadre urbain. Partant de l'hypothèse que, dans une décennie, la moitié des habitants de la planète vivront dans des villes, l'on peut affirmer que le jardin urbain contemporain est celui qui vole de l'espace au tissu constructif, qui s'en sert comme support ou occupe ses intérieurs. Les pages suivantes inventorient les solutions aussi singulières que des jardins grimpant aux façades, se nichant sur les toits ou occupant ces lieux résiduels entre les partitions ou la façade et la chaussée. Ces exemples prouvent que le jardin est aujourd'hui, plus que jamais, un lieu de compensation dans une dynamique urbaine frénétique, se convertissant en espace de décélération, de repos et de silence dans le tohu-bohu de la grande ville.

Le cadre urbain crée une série de déterminants clairs et complexes. Or ce sont souvent des petites touches individuelles qui aident à les résoudre avec subtilité. Il s'agit de pièces minimes de paysage, de dimensions architecturales, fonctionnant comme une acupuncture de la ville. Leurs avantages vont bien au-delà de ceux d'un jardin isolé. Leur caractère interstitiel les convertit en microcosmes participant à l'amélioration de la qualité de vie des urbains. Ce sont généralement

des jardins discrets, difficiles à résoudre et caractérisés par le « manque » : manque d'espace, de sol fertile, de temps ou de lumière. Cela se traduit par des limites très présentes et une dominante de matériaux durs face à l'élément végétal. Cependant, loin d'être exemplaires d'intentions inabouties, ce sont des démonstrations du génie humain appliqué aux situations de manque. Il s'agit d'un langage populaire, de lieux où le défaut essaye de se faire vertu, pour créer des jardins précisément où l'espace se révélait insuffisant pour les accueillir.

Le jardin, tel qu'il est présenté dans ce livre, se défend d'être un privilège réservé aux plus fortunés, voire aux propriétaires de terrains aux dimensions conséquentes. Il se convertit  plutôt en une opportunité offerte à tous ceux souhaitant recréer les processus naturels. Pour ce faire, les jardins se réduisent souvent à une portion congrue ou se mettent en valeur seulement par le biais d'allusions symboliques. C'est le cas des jardins éphémères, projets de jardins pour lesquels le concept de durabilité perd son importance. Ce sont fréquemment des installations paysagères occupant des lieux pendant un temps bref avec pour objectif de diriger le regard vers les particularités de l'endroit ou afin de lui ajouter de nouvelles interprétations. De ce fait, il est possible d'aboutir à l'expression minimale du jardin actuel : le pot de fleurs, propre des bords de fenêtre et balcons.

Les stratégies utilisées par les créateurs de par le monde soulignent les ressources pratiques nous rapprochant de cette tâche et nous enseignant que même ce conteneur traditionnel peut se convertir en une image suggestive de jardin de poche, ou « pocketgarden ». Des jardins qui, même pour les modèle de vie plus nomades, peuvent s'intégrer à ce quotidien d'asphalte et de béton que nous partageons pour la plupart.

Festival "Temps de Flors"(Flower Times), Girona 2001 by 10x15 col.lectiu
Photo © 10x15 col.lectiu

above: Patio of Can Girbal, Festival "Temps de Flors" (Flower Festival), Girona
below: "Embut de Llum" (Funnel of Light), Festival "Temps de Flors" (Flower Festival). Girona, photos © 10x15 col.lectiu

L a función que cumplen los jardines que se presentan en este libro, no difiere de aquellas que ha ejercido el jardín a lo largo de la historia. Los jardines se pueden clasificar en los de recreo y esparcimiento (locus amoenus, hortus ludi), los que asumen funciones de representatividad, los jardines-sala de exposición al aire libre o los meramente contemplativos (hortus contemplationis). Por otra parte, según el usuario, estos espacios se pueden clasificar en jardines privados, públicos o aquellos híbridos, que se encuentran entre los dos extremos. Aunque un jardín puede estar más o menos cargado de significación nunca deja de ser un espacio que proporciona a sus habitantes la ilusión de un dominio figurado en el que, al igual que en el paraíso, su existencia no se siente amenazada. La leyenda del jardín del Edén, tanto para musulmanes, cristianos o judíos, todavía forma parte de nuestro legado cultural, siendo responsable de actitudes y sentimientos del presente. Así mismo, los jardines son una señal indudable del interés que siempre ha experimentado el hombre hacia las plantas y la jardinería en general. El jardín ha estado y estará siempre ahí, al comienzo y al final de todos los procesos. Sin embargo, al margen de esta atemporalidad, en el presente libro se han querido destacar ejemplos de registros alternativos, poco convencionales o reinterpretaciones del jardín tradicional. La contemporaneidad de las diferentes propuestas expuestas aquí radica no solo en el empleo de nuevos materiales y técnicas constructivas sino, sobre todo, en un único común denominador: todos ellos son pequeños jardines en entornos urbanos. Partiendo de la hipótesis de que dentro de una década la mitad de los habitantes del planeta viviremos en ciudades, se puede afirmar que el jardín urbano contemporáneo es aquel que roba espacio al tejido edificado, que lo usa como soporte y que ocupa sus interiores. En las siguientes páginas se recogen soluciones tan singulares como jardines que trepan por las fachadas, los que anidan sobre los tejados o los que ocupan esos lugares residuales entre medianeras o entre la fachada y la calzada. Estos ejemplos evidencian que el jardín es ahora más que nunca un lugar de compensación dentro de la frenética dinámica urbana, convirtiéndose en espacios de desaceleración, reposo y silencio dentro del bullicio de la gran ciudad.

El entorno urbano crea una serie de determinantes claras y complejas y a menudo son las pequeñas acciones individuales las que ayudan a resolverlas con sutileza. Se trata de piezas mínimas de paisaje, de dimensiones arquitectónicas, y que funcionan a modo de acupuntura en la ciudad. Sus beneficios van más allá de los propios de un jardín aislado. El carácter intersticial los convierte en microcosmos que ayudan a mejorar la calidad de vida de los habitantes de la

urbe. En general son jardines discretos, difíciles de resolver y caracterizados por "la falta": la falta de espacio, la falta de suelo fértil, la falta de tiempo o la falta de luz. Todo ello se traduce en una fuerte presencia de sus límites y en un predominio de materiales duros frente al elemento vegetal. Sin embargo, lejos de ser ejemplos de intenciones no logradas son auténticas muestras de uso del ingenio en situaciones de falta de recursos. Se trata, en lenguaje popular, de lugares en los que alguien ha intentado hacer de un defecto una virtud, logrando jardines allá donde prácticamente no había espacio para ellos.

El jardín tal y como se presenta en este libro, lejos de ser un privilegio reservado a las clases más adineradas, o a aquellas personas que disponen de una parcela de dimensiones considerables, se convierte en una oportunidad al alcance de la mano de cualquiera de recrear los procesos naturales. Para lograrlo muchas veces los jardines se reducen a unos mínimos o se evidencian tan solo a través de alusiones simbólicas. Tal es el caso de los jardines efímeros, proyectos de jardines en los que el concepto de durabilidad carece de importancia. Se trata en general de instalaciones de jardines que ocupan lugares durante un corto espacio de tiempo con el objetivo de dirigir la mirada hacia las particularidades del sitio o para añadir nuevas interpretaciones del mismo. De esta manera se podría llegar hasta la expresión mínima del jardín actual: la maceta, propia de los alféizares y balcones.

Las estrategias utilizadas por diseñadores en todo el mundo evidencian los recursos prácticos que nos acercan a esta labor y nos enseñan que incluso este tradicional contenedor se puede convertir en una sugerente imagen de jardín de bolsillo o "pocketgarden". Jardines que hasta en los modelos de vida más nómadas pueden llegar a incorporarse a esta cotidianidad de asfalto y hormigón que la mayoría de nosotros compartimos.

Plantpack by Paula Hayes
Photo © Warren Weidich

1 Toronto (Canada)
2 New York (USA)
3 Tolima (Colombia)
4 Curitiba (Brasil)
5 Mallorca (Spain)
6 Barcelona (Spain)
  Sabadell (Spain)
  Sant Cugat del Vallès (Spain)
7 Paris (France)
  Cordes-sur-ciel (France)
  Albi-Rodez (France)
  Eygalières (France)
8 Wintherthur (Switzerland)
  Küsnacht (Switzerland)
9 Venice (Italy)
10 Carnate (Italy)
11 Aartselaar (Belgium)
12 Rotterdam (Netherlands)
13 Hamburg (Germany)
14 Berlin (Germany)
15 Salzburg (Austria)
   Vienna (Austria)
16 Copenhagen (Denmark)
17 Osaka (Japan)
18 Tokyo (Japan)
19 Sydney (Australia)
20 Adelaide (Australia)

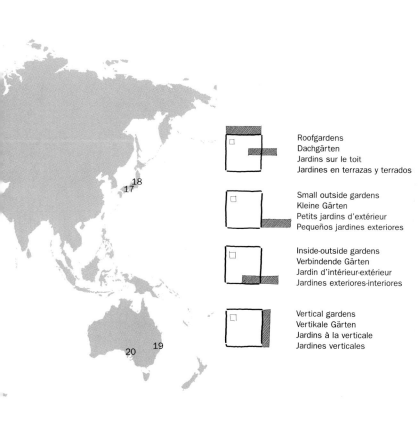

Roofgardens
Dachgärten
Jardins sur le toit
Jardines en terrazas y terrados

Small outside gardens
Kleine Gärten
Petits jardins d'extérieur
Pequeños jardines exteriores

Inside-outside gardens
Verbindende Gärten
Jardin d'intérieur-extérieur
Jardines exteriores-interiores

Vertical gardens
Vertikale Gärten
Jardins à la verticale
Jardines verticales

The limited dimensions of the space occupied by this garden meant that some of the plants had to be integrated into its boundaries: a Mermaid rose covers the brick wall, a bamboo fence separates the garden from the street and a star-shaped jasmine climbs over the railings. The rest of the vegetation comprises more than thirty species of aromatic plants, mostly for culinary use, which blossom in rotation over the course of the year. In contrast with the diversity of the vegetation, the only materials used are sand, in warm colors, and a few railroad sleepers, which divide the plant beds in a radial pattern around one of the building's pillars.

Aufgrund der geringen Ausmaße des als Garten nutzbaren Raumes wurde dort zwangsläufig ein Teil der Pflanzen untergebracht. Eine „Mermaid"-Rose bedeckt die Backsteinmauer, eine Bambuspflanzung trennt den Garten von der Straße und ein Jasminstrauch rankt sich den Zaun empor. In einem weiteren Bereich befindet sich eine Anpflanzung von über dreißig Arten von aromatischen Pflanzen, die meisten davon Gewürzpflanzen. Die Blütezeiten wechseln sich übers Jahr ab. Im Gegensatz zu der Pflanzenvielfalt ist die Auswahl an Baustoffen auf Eisenbahnschwellen beschränkt, welche strahlenförmig um einen Gebäudepfeiler angeordnet liegen und zusammen mit Sand in warmen Farbtönen den Boden gliedern.

Les limites mêmes de l'espace réduit destiné au jardin ont du être mises à profit pour supporter une partie de la végétation choisie. Une rose « Mermaid » recouvre le mur de brique, une haie de bambou sépare le jardin de la rue et un jasmin étoilé grimpe le long de la grille. La seconde proposition végétale inclut plus de trente espèces de plantes aromatiques, dont la plupart à usage culinaire. Les floraisons alternent tout au long de l'année. Contrastant avec la diversité des plantes, les matériaux employés se réduisent à des traverses de voies ferrées organisant les parterres en rayon autour d'un pilier de l'édifice et de sable aux tons chauds.

Las reducidas dimensiones del espacio destinado a jardín han obligado a utilizar los mismos como soporte para una parte de la elección vegetal. Una rosa "Mermaid" recubre el muro de ladrillo, una valla de bambú separa el jardín de la calle y un jazmín estrellado trepa por la verja. La segunda apuesta vegetal incluye más de treinta especies de plantas aromáticas, la mayoría de las cuales son de uso culinario. Las floraciones se alternan a lo largo del año. En contraste con la variedad de plantas, los materiales empleados se reducen a unas traviesas de tren para organizar los parterres de forma radial en torno a un pilar del edificio y arena de tonos cálidos.

# Lola Farré's Garden

### Design: Carme Farré, biologist and landscape gardener

Location: **Sant Cugat del Vallès, Spain**
Construction date: **2000**
Photos: © **Alejandro Bahamón**

This holiday retreat for three business partners is set in two former colonial houses; these had previously been converted, although the existing walls and some of the original configuration were retained. The house is a succession of spaces—some open, others only partly open or enclosed—bounded by the old colonial walls and some newer additions. These spaces are connected by a series of patios and gardens dominated by various elements: wood, natural stone, gravel, aromatic plants, palms, fruit trees and a range of ornamental plants. This diversity is unified by the presence of water, found in the form of thin ponds and channels, or splashing from the fountains designed by the architects.

Dieses Ferienhaus für drei Geschäftspartner befindet sich auf einem Grundstück mit zwei zuvor instand gesetzten Häusern im Kolonialstil, von denen die vorhandenen Mauern und einige Originalräume erhalten wurden. Das Haus besteht aus einer Abfolge von offenen, halboffenen und überdachten Räumen, die von den erhaltenen Kolonialmauern und den neu errichteten Mauern umgeben sind. Sie sind durch eine Reihe von unterschiedlich gestalteten Innenhöfen und Gärten verbunden: Holz, Naturstein, Kies, Kräuter, Palmen, Obstbäume und verschiedene Arten von Zierpflanzen. Hinzu kommt das auf verschiedene Arten eingesetzte Wasser, das als Film herabfließt, in Kanälen strömt oder aus von den Architekten selbst gestalteten Brunnen quillt.

Cette maison de loisirs pour trois associés est implantée dans deux anciennes maisons coloniales, ayant fait l'objet d'une intervention, dont les murs coloniaux existants et quelques espaces originaux ont été préservés. La maison est une succession d'espaces ouverts, semi ouverts et couverts, formés par ces murs coloniaux et les nouvelles cloisons, et interconnectés par des patios et jardins aux traitements divers : bois, pierre naturelle, gravier, plantes aromatiques, palmiers, arbres fruitiers et plantes ornementales de tout type. S'y ajoute la présence de l'eau, apparaissant en flaques, canaux ou jaillissant de sources conçues par les architectes eux-mêmes.

Esta casa de recreo para tres socios está implantada en dos antiguas casas coloniales, previamente intervenidas, de las que se conservaron los muros coloniales existentes y algunos espacios originales. La casa es una sucesión de espacios abiertos, semiabiertos y cubiertos, conformados por los muros coloniales preservados y los nuevos muros, y conectados a través de una serie de patios y jardines con diferentes tratamientos: madera, piedra natural, grava, plantas aromáticas, palmeras, árboles frutales y plantas ornamentales de diferente tipo. A ello se le une la presencia del agua, que aparece a modo de lámina, canales o bien brotando de fuentes diseñadas por los mismos arquitectos.

# House in Honda

**Design: Guillermo Arias Villa and Luis Cuartas Giraldo, architects**

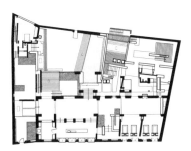

Elevation plan 1

Location: **Honda (Tolima), Colombia**

Construction date: **2000**

Photos: © **Eduardo Consuegra**

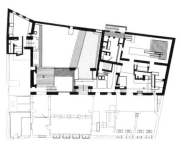

Elevation plan 2

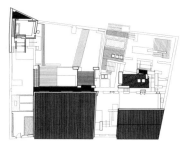

Elevation plan 3

Syoasai-kan is an old stationery store. The garden is set in the entrance to the store and aims to evoke a sense of calm in the midst of the noisy hubbub of the city; it serves as both a private garden and public space. Various motifs typical of a Japanese garden rub shoulders with more Western elements, creating a fusion between the Japanese and European sensibilities. So, the zigzag intrinsic to Zen gardens—here marked out in pink granite—sets off the Turkish-style stone bench overlooking a pool of water. The vegetation is made up of *Ophiopogon*, between the flagstones, *Lagestroemia indica* (a profusely blossoming tree), *Papyrus* and *Equisetum hyemale*.

Syoasai-kan ist ein altes Schreibwarengeschäft. Der Garten befindet sich am Eingang des Ladens und soll innerhalb der ihn umgebenden Geräuschkulisse der Stadt ein Gefühl von Ruhe vermitteln. Er soll gleichzeitig Privatgarten und öffentlicher Raum sein. Verschiedene Motive der japanischen Gartengestaltung wechseln sich mit eher westlichen Techniken ab und lassen so die japanische und die westliche Empfindungswelt verschmelzen. Auf diese Weise geht das Zickzack der Zen-Gärten, das hier durch rosa Granit vertreten ist, einen Dialog mit einer türkisch inspirierten Steinbank über einer Wasserfläche ein. Die Vegetation besteht aus *Ophiopogon* zwischen den Steinplatten, *Lagestroemia indica* (kräftig blühender Baum), *Papyrus und Equisetum hyemale*.

Syoasai-kan est une ancienne papeterie. Le jardin se situe à l'entrée de la boutique et veut évoquer les sensations de tranquillité dans le cadre urbain bruyant qui l'entoure, tenant lieu à la fois de jardin privé et d'espace public. Différents motifs propres au jardin japonais alternent avec des techniques plus occidentales, créant une fusion entre les sensibilités japonaise et européenne. Ainsi, le zigzag propre aux jardins zen, ici représenté par le granite rose, dialogue avec un banc de pierre d'influence turque disposé sur une superficie aquatique. La végétation est composée d'*Ophiopogon* entre les dalles de pierre, de *Lagestroemia indica* (arbre fleurissant à foison), de *Papyrus et d'Equisetum hyemale*.

Syoasai-kan es una antigua papelería. El jardín se ubica en la entrada de la tienda y pretende evocar sensaciones de tranquilidad en el ruidoso ambiente urbano que lo rodea, ejerciendo a la vez de jardín privado y espacio público. Diferentes motivos propios del jardín japonés se alternan con técnicas más occidentales, creando una fusión entre la sensibilidad japonesa y la europea. Así, el zig-zag propio de los jardines zen y que aquí aparece representado por el granito rosa dialoga con un banco de piedra de influencia turca colocado sobre una superficie de agua. La vegetación está compuesta por *Ophiopogon* entre las losas de piedra, *Lagestroemia indica* (árbol de potente floración), *Papyrus* y *Equisetum hyemale*.

# Syoasai-kan

**Design: Yoji Sasaki, landscape architect, and Mikio Yasui, architect**

Location: **Tokyo, Japan**
Construction date: **1999**
Photos: © **Kazuaki Hosokawa**

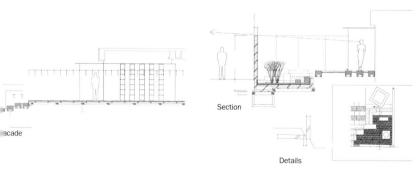

Section

Details

acade

Here the aim was to turn an old industrial courtyard into a green space for homes and offices. The project had to respond to two different types of demands: the functional requirements of the offices and the leisure needs of the residents. An asphalt passageway linking the entrance to the patio with the offices forms a linear element around which the garden is organized. Other secondary paths and the rest of the spaces contrast with this axis as regards materials, form and directionality. A lively interplay of colors and lines sets up a dialog between the garden and the facades to turn this shady patio into a spot replete with light and movement.

Ziel war die Umgestaltung eines alten Fabrikinnenhofes in eine Grünzone für Wohnungen und Büros. Das Projekt berücksichtigt zwei verschiedene Ansprüche: die Bedürfnisse nach eher repräsentativer Gestaltung für die Büros und diejenigen der Bewohner nach Freizeitgestaltung. Ein asphaltierter Weg, der den Hofeingang mit den Büros verbindet, bildet die lineare Struktur, um die der Garten angordnet ist. Weitere sekundäre Wege sowie die übrigen Räume stehen zu dieser Achse im Kontrast in Bezug auf Materialien, Formen und Ausrichtungen. Verschiedene Farbspiele und Linien schaffen einen Dialog zwischen dem Garten und den Fassaden und machen diesen schattigen Garten zu einem Ort der Bewegung und des Lichts.

L'objectif était de transformer un ancien patio industriel en un espace vert pour logements et bureaux. Le projet répond à deux types différents de demande : les besoins les plus représentatifs des bureaux et le plaisir des résidents. Un cheminement asphalté unissant l'entrée du patio aux bureaux constitue la structure linéaire autour de laquelle s'organise le jardin. D'autres voies de circulation secondaires et le reste de l'espace contrastent avec cet axe quant aux matériaux, formes et directions. Divers jeux chromatiques et lignes établissent un dialogue entre le jardin et les façades pour convertir ce patio sombre en un lieu de mouvement et de lumière.

El objetivo ha consistido en transformar un antiguo patio industrial en un espacio verde para viviendas y oficinas. El proyecto responde a dos tipos de demandas diferentes: las necesidades más representativas de las oficinas y las propias del disfrute de los habitantes. Un pasillo asfaltado que une la entrada al patio con las oficinas constituye la estructura lineal entorno a la cual se organiza el jardín. Otras circulaciones secundarias y el resto de los espacios contrastan con este eje en cuanto a materiales, formas y direccionalidad. Diferentes juegos cromáticos y líneas establecen un diálogo entre el jardín y las fachadas y convierten este patio sombrío en un lugar de movimiento y luz.

# Patio in Berlin-Kreuzberg

## Design: Levin Monsigny, landscape architects

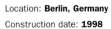

Location: **Berlin, Germany**
Construction date: **1998**
Photos: © **Claas Dreppenstedt / Levin Monsigny**
Sculptures: **Werner Keller**

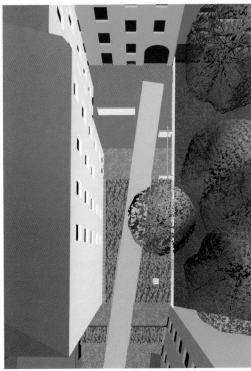

Perspective drawing

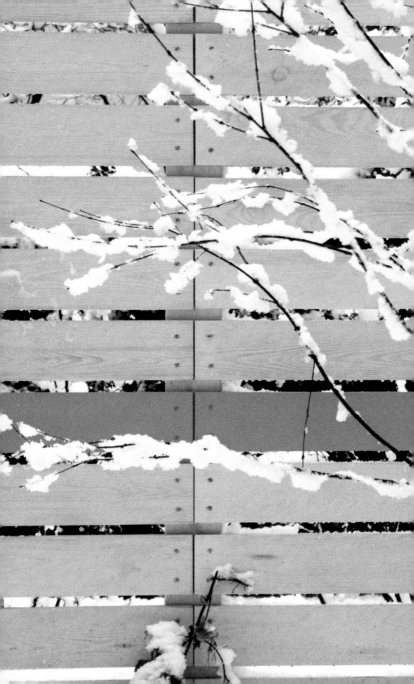

The "Walking on Water" project illustrates how a small space can be made compatible with a number of different functions. This patio is intended to serve for parking, for relaxing and for gaining access to the house. It is made up of a series of steps and walkways set inside a pit that can be totally or partially flooded. A high level of water can rule out certain uses, to the extent that it becomes an unavoidable obstacle between the street and the house. *Phyllostachys nigra*, *Wisteria sinensis*, *Raphis excelsa* and *Bambusa multiplex* are some of the plants that have been chosen.

Das Projek „Walking on Water" ist ein Lösungsbeispiel für einen Raum mit geringen Ausmaßen und verschiedenen Nutzungsmöglichkeiten. Dieser Innenhof soll gleichzeitig Park- und Aufenthaltsraum sein sowie Zugang zu Fuß zum Wohnraum ermöglichen. Er besteht aus einer Reihe von Stufen und Laufstegen, die sich in einem ganz oder teilweise überflutbaren Graben befinden. Je nach Wasserstand sind eine oder mehrere Nutzungsmöglichkeiten ausgeschlossen und können sogar zu einem symbolisch unüberwindbaren Hindernis auf dem Weg zwischen Fahrbahn und Haus werden. Für die Bepflanzung wurden unter anderem *Phyllostachys nigra*, *Wisteria sinensis*, *Raphis excelsa* und *Bambusa multiplex* gewählt.

Le projet « Walking on Water » est un exemple du mode de solution d'un espace aux dimensions réduites pour accueillir divers usages. Ce patio doit être à la fois un lieu pour se garer, pour séjourner ou à parcourir pour accéder à la maison. Les éléments qui le forment sont une série d'échelons et de sentiers, situés dans une fosse, inondable en tout ou partie. Selon le niveau atteint par l'eau, certains usages sont exclus, ou non, pour se convertir même en un obstacle symbolique infranchissable entre la route et la maison. Le choix de végétation inclut *Phyllostachys nigra*, *Wisteria sinensis*, *Raphis excelsa* et *Bambusa multiplex*.

El proyecto "Walking on Water" es un ejemplo de como solucionar un espacio de reducidas dimensiones para llegar a albergar diferentes usos. Este patio tiene que ser a la vez un lugar donde aparcar y un lugar de estar o por el que caminar para acceder a la vivienda. Los elementos que lo conforman son una serie de escalones y paseras, ubicados dentro de una fosa, parcial o totalmente inundable. Según el nivel que alcanza el agua se excluyen unos u otros usos, llegando a convertirse hasta en un simbólico obstáculo insalvable entre la calzada y la casa. La elección de la vegetación incluye *Phyllostachys nigra*, *Wisteria sinensis*, *Raphis excelsa* y *Bambusa multiplex*.

# Walking on Water
### Design: Terragram Pty. Ltd., landscape architects

Location: **Sydney, Australia**
Construction date: **1999**
Photos: © **Walter Glover, Terragram Pty. Ltd.**

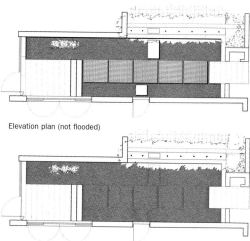

Elevation plan (not flooded)

Elevation plan (flooded)

Hakuu-Kan is a residential complex with white walls that interlink to form a series of open spaces of various kinds: a parking lot, a sand garden and various secondary court-yards. The project was based around the changing properties of light, color, wind and water, in order to bring the inhabitants of the complex into closer contact with nature. The vegetation is made up of *Equisetum*, *Bamboo*, *Ophiopogon* and *Acer palmatum*. During the day the colors and textures of the vegetation set up a dialogue with the construction materials (concrete, stone, glass, etc.), while at night the lighting changes the character of the setting completely.

Hakuu-Kan ist ein Wohnkomplex, in dem weiße Mauern eine Reihe von offenen Räumen unterschiedlicher Arten bilden: Parkplatz, Sandgarten und mehrere zweitrangige Innenhö-fe. Die Projektgestaltung beruht auf den wandlungsfähigen Eigenschaften von Licht, Farbe, Wind und Wasser, um so Naturerfahrungen in das Leben der Bewohner zu integrieren. Die Bepflanzung besteht aus *Equisetum*, *Bamboo*, *Ophiopogon* und *Acer palmatum*. Tagsüber treten die Farben und Stofflichkeiten in einen Dialog mit denen der baulichen Komponen-ten (Beton, Stein, Glas, usw.) und während der Nacht verleiht die Beleuchtung dem Kom-plex einen vollkommen andersartigen Charakter.

Hakuu-Kan est un complexe résidentiel où des murs blancs s'entrelacent pour former une série d'espaces ouverts de différentes typologies : zone de stationnement, parc à sa-ble et divers patios secondaires. Le projet repose sur les qualités changeantes de la lu-mière, la couleur, le vent et l'eau, afin d'introduire des expériences naturelles dans la vie des habitants de la résidence. La végétation comprend *Equisetum*, *Bamboo*, *Ophiopogon* et *Acer palmatum*. Dans la journée, les couleurs de la végétation dialoguent avec les élé-ments constructifs eux-mêmes (béton, pierre, verre, etc.) et la nuit, l'éclairage donne un caractère complètement différent à l'ensemble.

Hakuu-Kan es un complejo residencial en el que unos muros blancos se entrelazan for-mando una serie de espacios abiertos de diferentes tipologías: zona de aparcamiento, jar-dín de arena y varios patios secundarios. El proyecto ha sido concebido sobre la base de las cualidades mutables de la luz, el color, el viento y el agua, con el fin de introducir ex-periencias naturales en la vida de los habitantes del complejo. La vegetación está com-puesta por *Equisetum*, *Bamboo*, *Ophiopogon*, y *Acer palmatum*. Durante el día los colores y las texturas de la vegetación dialogan con aquellos propios de los elementos construc-tivos (hormigón, piedra, cristal, etcétera), y durante la noche la iluminación da un carácter completamente diferente al conjunto.

# Hakuu-Kan

**Design: Yoji Sasaki, landscape architect, Akira Sakamoto, architect**

Location: **Osaka, Japan**
Construction date: **1999**
Photos: © **Kei Sugino**

Perspective drawing

Elevation plan

With this project Topotek 1 had to come up with solutions for two types of space: a sunny terrace and a shady inner courtyard. The result was two sharply differentiated spaces that nevertheless both share the attribute of a circular element that reflects the sky. In the inner courtyard a fountain at ground level introduces the sound of running water, which combines with the creeping ivy and the dark tiles to convey the impression of a grotto. The communal terrace is equipped with benches, a table and a sandpit, while the rubber flooring means that children can use the entire space to play.

Mit diesem Projekt verfolgt Topotek 1 das Ziel, eine Antwort auf zwei unterschiedliche Raumtypen zu geben: eine sonnige Terrasse und einen schattigen Innenhof. Das Resultat sind zwei unterschiedliche Räume, deren Gemeinsamkeit ein kreisförmiges Element bildet, in dem sich der Himmel spiegelt. Im Innenhof bringt ein Brunnen zu ebener Erde das Geräusch des Wassers an einen Ort, der zusammen mit einem Kletterefeu und der dunklen Farbe des Bodens wie ein Grotte wirkt. Auf der Gemeinschaftsterrasse befinden sich Bänke, ein Tisch und ein Sandkasten. Dank eines Bodenbelags aus Gummi können hier Kinder spielen.

Topotek 1 avait comme objectif pour ce projet d'apporter une réponse à deux typologies d'espaces : une terrasse ensoleillée et un patio obscur. Il en est résulté deux lieux différenciés ayant en commun la présence d'un élément circulaire dans lequel se reflète le ciel. Dans le patio intérieur, une source située au ras du sol apporte le son de l'eau à un endroit qui, sous l'influence du lierre grimpant et des tons obscurs du sol, acquiert un caractère caverneux. La terrasse commune incorpore les éléments suivants : des bancs, une table et une sablière. Le revêtement en gomme permet à l'espace de s'offrir aux jeux des enfants.

El objetivo de Topotek 1 para este proyecto consiste en dar respuesta a dos tipologías de espacios: una terraza soleada y un patio interior sombrío. El resultado son dos lugares diferenciados que tienen en común la presencia de un elemento circular en el que se refleja el cielo. En el patio interior una fuente de agua a ras del suelo aporta el sonido del agua a un lugar que con la presencia de hiedra trepadora y el color oscuro del suelo adquiere un carácter de gruta. La terraza comunitaria incorpora bancos, una mesa y un arenero. El pavimento de goma permite el uso del espacio como lugar de juegos infantiles.

# arden in Hackescher Markt

**Design: TOPOTEK 1, landscape architects**

Location: **Berlin, Germany**
Construction date: **2000**
Photos: **© Hanns Joosten**

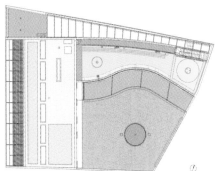

Elevation plan

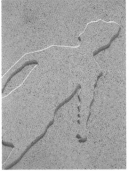

The Higashigaoka garden in the centre of Tokyo is divided into three distinct spaces. The "entrance/reception garden" boasts a series of ornamental trees (*Lagestroemia indica*), perimeter flower beds and tubs with hedges that provide a degree of privacy. The "meeting garden" is set below the first garden. In the center a geometrical fountain serves as a refrigerator for drinks in summer, when the residents use this area to hold parties. Finally, two small courtyards of a symbolic nature are set in the central part of the residential complex: the "moon courtyard" and the "vega courtyard".

Der Higashigaoka-Garten im Zentrum von Tokio ist in drei verschiedenartige Räume unterteilt: Der „Empfangs- oder Eingangsgarten" besteht aus einer Abfolge von Zierbäumen (*Lagestroemia indica*), umlaufenden Blumenpflanzungen und Gartenkübeln mit Hecken, die eine gewissen Privatsphäre schaffen. Der „Begegnungsgarten" ist im Verhältnis zum vorherigen tiefer gelegen. Der geometrische Brunnen in seiner Mitte dient im Sommer zur Kühlung von Getränken, da die Bewohner diesen Raum für Festlichkeiten nutzen. Schließlich fügen sich noch zwei kleine Gärten mit symbolischem Charakter in das Mittelstück des Wohnkomplexes ein: der „Mondhof" und der „Vega-Hof".

Le jardin de Higashigaoka, situé au cœur de Tokyo, est divisé en trois typologies d'espace différentes : le « jardin réceptacle ou entrée » présente une séquence d'arbres ornementaux (*Lagestroemia indica*), de plantations périphériques de fleurs, des jardinières avec des haies conférant à l'endroit une certaine intimité. Le « jardin de réunion » se trouve enfoui en regard du jardin précédent. En son centre, une source géométrique est utilisée en été pour refroidir les boissons, les résidents profitant du lieu pour organiser des fêtes. Enfin, deux petits patios au caractère symbolique s'intègrent à la pièce centrale du complexe résidentiel : le « patio de la lune » et le « patio vega ».

El jardín de Higashigaoka, ubicado en el centro de Tokio, está dividido en tres tipologías de espacios diferentes: El "jardín recibidor o de entrada" presenta una secuencia de árboles ornamentales (*Lagestroemia indica*), plantaciones perimetrales de flores y jardineras con setos que consiguen otorgar una cierta privacidad. El "jardín de reunión" se encuentra hundido respecto al jardín anterior. En su centro una fuente geométrica se utiliza en verano como refrigerador de bebidas, ya que los residentes utilizan este espacio para hacer fiestas. Por último, dos patios pequeños de carácter simbólico se incorporan a la pieza central del complejo residencial: el "patio de la luna" y el "patio vega".

# Higashigaoka Garden

**Design: Yoji Sasaki, landscape architect, and Mikio Yasui, architect**

Location: **Tokyo, Japan**
Construction date: **1999**
Photos: © **Kazuaki Hosokawa**

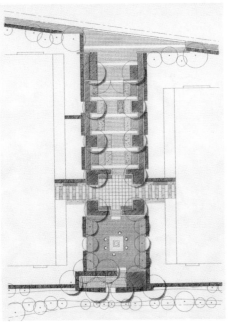

Elevation plan

The aim of this project was to give a new twist to the idea of the patio in a Mediterranean house by turning the ground floor of a residential block into an oasis of green in the heart of the city. The various elements that make up the patio are laid out in sharply defined areas, with the vegetation spread along the edges of the patio and separated by a strip of gravel from the floored area, which, like the benches, is made of IP tropical wood. The vegetation is made up of the following species: *Phyllostachys aurea, Parthenocissus tricuspidata, Ficus repens, Pittosporum tobira nana, Abelia floribunda, Photinia serrulata, Cersis siliquastrum, Adiantum, Nephrolepis* and *Begonia.*

Die Absicht des Projekts ist es, den Gedanken des mediterranen Hauses mit Innenhof wieder aufzunehmen und das Untergeschoss eines Wohnhauses in eine grüne Oase mitten im Stadtzentrum zu verwandeln. Die verschiedenen Elemente des Innenhofes sind klar aufgeteilt. Die Bepflanzung ist entlang der Umfangsmauer des Innenhofes verteilt und ein Kiesstreifen trennt sie von der Holzterrasse. Diese besteht wie auch die Bänke aus tropischem IP-Holz. Die Bepflanzung besteht aus folgenden Spezies: *Phyllostachys aurea, Parthenocissus tricuspidata, Ficus repens, Pittosporum tobira nana, Abelia floribunda, Photinia serrulata, Cersis siliquastrum, Adiantum, Nephrolepis* und *Begonia.*

L'intention du projet était de récupérer l'idée de la maison patio méditerranéenne, transformant le rez-de-chaussée d'un immeuble de logements en oasis de verdure au cœur de la ville. La distribution des différents éléments composant le patio est claire, la végétation étant répartie le long de son périmètre et une frange de gravier le sépare du parquet de bois. Ce dernier, comme les bancs, est en bois tropical d'IP. La végétation comprend les espèces suivantes : *Phyllostachys aurea, Parthenocissus tricuspidata, Ficus repens, Pittosporum tobira nana, Abelia floribunda, Photinia serrulata, Cersis siliquastrum, Adiantum, Nephrolepis* et *Begonia.*

La intención del proyecto es recuperar la idea de la casa patio mediterránea, convirtiendo la planta baja de un edificio de viviendas en un oasis verde en pleno centro de la ciudad. La distribución de los diferentes elementos que componen el patio es clara, la vegetación se encuentra repartida a lo largo del perímetro del patio y una franja de grava la separa del entarimado de madera. Este último, igual que los bancos, es de madera tropical de IP. La vegetación está compuesta por las siguientes especies: *Phyllostachys aurea, Parthenocissus tricuspidata, Ficus repens, Pittosporum tobira nana, Abelia floribunda, Photinia serrulata, Cersis siliquastrum, Adiantum, Nephrolepis* y *Begonia.*

# Patio in Barcelona

Design: Magda Sunyer, landscape architect, Jordi Romeu, architect

Location: **Barcelona, Spain**
Construction date: **2002**
Photos: © **Alejandro Bahamón**

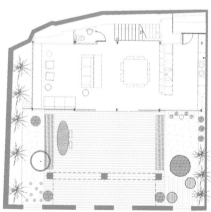

Elevation plan

The sculptor Rae Bolotin commissioned PSB to convert a small, overrun private garden on extremely uneven terrain into an art gallery. The design meets this challenge with a combination of concrete steps, platforms, balustrades, benches, bridges and walls. The result is a labyrinth that, paradoxically, reduces the topographical complexity of the site. The new gallery gives the art works great freedom to express themselves. The character of each space is defined by the use of different materials for the flooring and plants, and walls in colors that contrast with the rocky outcrops and the vegetation in the surrounding lots.

Der Auftrag an PSB für den Bildhauer Rae Bolotin bestand darin, einen kleinen und verwilderten Privatgarten mit komplizierter Topografie in eine Ausstellungsgalerie zu verwandeln. Die gestalterische Lösung besteht im Abwechseln von Betontreppen, Plattformen, Balustraden, Bänken, Brücken und Mauern. Als Ergebnis entstand ein Labyrinth, das paradoxerweise die topografische Komplexität des Ortes reduziert. Die neu entstandene Galerie bietet den ausgestellten Werken breitgefächerte Ausdrucksmöglichkeiten. Jeder der Ausstellungsräume wird durch den Einsatz unterschiedlicher Materialien für Bodenbelag, Bepflanzungen und Mauerfarben bestimmt, die mit den Felsformationen, der Vegetation und der Aufteilung der Umgebung kontrastieren.

Convertir un petit jardin sylvestre particulier à la topographie complexe en une grande galerie d'exposition, tel fut la commande du sculpteur Rae Bolotin à PSB. Le design répond par une grande alternance d'escaliers de béton, de plates-formes, de balustrades, de bancs, de ponts et de murs. Le résultat en est un labyrinthe simplifiant paradoxalement la topographie du lieu. La nouvelle galerie offre aux œuvres une grande marge d'expression. Le caractère de chaque espace est défini par l'emploi de différents matériaux de revêtement, de plantations et de couleurs de mur contrastant avec les affleurements rocheux, la végétation et la parcellisation du cadre.

Convertir un pequeño y asilvestrado jardín particular de complicada topografía en una galería de exposición fue el encargo que el escultor Rae Bolotin hizo a PSB. El diseño responde con una alternancia de escaleras de hormigón, plataformas, balaustradas, bancos, puentes y muros. El resultado es un laberinto que paradójicamente reduce la complejidad topográfica del lugar. La nueva galería ofrece a las obras un amplio margen de expresión. El carácter de cada uno de los espacios se define mediante el empleo de diferentes materiales de pavimentación, plantaciones y colores de muros que contrastan con los afloramientos rocosos, la vegetación y la parcelación del entorno.

# ane Cove Sculpture Garden

Design: Pittendrigh Shinkfield Bruce, (PSB) Jon Shinkfield,
landscape architects and urban designers

Location: **Lane Cove, Sydney, Australia**
Construction date: **2002**
Photos: © **Anthony Browell**

This patio to the rear of the RSCO offices is dominated by the balls of Carrara marble cemented to the wall. The same material is spread over the floor to serve as paving, thereby creating continuity between the two planes. The whiteness and crystalline structure of the stone reflect the light entering from the exterior and project it into the kitchen and the conference room. The patio also enhances the ventilation of the building. The long bench is made up of sixteen prefabricated concrete slabs and eight U-shape steel elements. The only vertical element in the patio is a 19 feet high column.

Der Innenhof liegt am Ende der Büros von RSCO und besteht aus Flusssteinen aus Carrara-Marmor, die mit Mörtel an der Wand befestigt sind. Auf dem Boden setzt sich dasselbe Material als Bepflasterung fort und schafft so eine Kontinuität zwischen den beiden Ebenen. Die weiße Farbe und die kristalline Struktur des Steins reflektieren das Licht von außen und leiten es in die Küche und den Sitzungsraum weiter. Auf die gleiche Art wird das Gebäude belüftet. Die kleine längliche Bank besteht aus sechzehn Fertigbetonplatten und acht U-förmig angeordneten Stahlelementen. Das einzige vertikale Element des Innenhofes ist eine 5,7 m hohe Säule.

Le patio, situé au fond des bureaux de RSCO, est composé de boules de marbre de Carrare rondes, fixées au mur à l'aide de mortier. Au sol, le même matériau s'étend tel un revêtement, créant une continuité entre les deux plans. La couleur blanche et la structure cristalline de la pierre reflètent la lumière extérieure, la projetant vers la cuisine et la salle de conférence. La ventilation de l'immeuble naît de la même façon. Le petit banc allongé est formé de seize carreaux de béton préfabriqué et de huit éléments d'acier en U. L'unique élément vertical du patio est un pilier de 5,7 m.

El patio, ubicado al fondo de las oficinas RSCO está compuesto por bolos de rio de mármol de Carrara fijadas mediante mortero a la pared. En el suelo, el mismo material se extiende a modo de pavimento, creando un continuo entre ambos planos. El color blanco y la estructura cristalina de la piedra reflejan la luz del exterior proyectándola hacia la cocina y la sala de conferencias. De la misma manera se facilita la ventilación del edificio. El pequeño banco alargado está formado por dieciséis baldosas de hormigón prefabricado y ocho elementos de acero en U. El único elemento vertical del patio es un pilar de 5,7 m.

# Patio RSCO Office

### Design: Jan Bleys, landscape architect

Location: **Aartselaar, Belgium**
Construction date: **2001**
Photos: © **Niels Donckers**

Ground floor

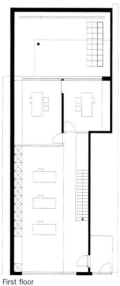

First floor

■ The foremost aim of the courtyards in the Gruner+Jahr office complex was the creation of a physical reference point for the users of the building (over two thousand in all). Wood, stone and a restricted selection of plants are the basic elements. Balancing the built-up space and the open areas was the main challenge, so a special effort was made to differentiate each courtyard from all the others. This makes it easier to find one's way around the complex, as the different work spaces are identified with a specific courtyard. Due to the large scale of the project, only a limited number of the courtyards are shown here.

■ Der Entwurf der Innenhöfe für den Bürokomplex von Gruner+Jahr soll vor allem Bezugspunkt für die über zweitausend Benutzer sein. Holz, Stein und eine reduzierte Auswahl von Pflanzen sind Grundlage des Entwurfs. Einen Ausgleich zwischen bebautem und freiem Raum herzustellen, gehört zu den wichtigsten Aspekten. Auf der anderen Seite wurde besonderer Wert darauf gelegt, durch deutliche Unterscheidung der einzelnen Innenhöfe die Orientierung innerhalb des Bürokomplexes zu erleichtern. Hierdurch entsteht die jeweilige Identifizierung der verschiedenen Arbeitsbereiche mit einem ganz konkreten Innenhof. Aufgrund der Ausmaße des Projekts wird nur eine Auswahl von einigen Innenhöfen gezeigt.

■ Le projet des patios du complexe de bureaux de Gruner+Jahr se veut avant tout une référence physique pour les plus de deux mille usagers. Bois, pierre et un choix limité de plantes sont la base du projet. Compenser l'occupation de l'espace construit et l'espace libre est un des principaux objectifs poursuivis. D'un autre côté, et pour faciliter l'orientation dans le complexe de bureaux, l'accent a été porté sur la différenciation de chacun des patios restants. Ainsi les différents lieux de travail sont identifiés par un patio précis. De par la magnitude du projet, seuls quelques patios choisis sont présentés.

■ El proyecto de los patios del complejo de oficinas de Gruner+Jahr busca ante todo ser una referencia física para los más de dos mil usuarios. Madera, piedra y una selección limitada de plantas son la base del proyecto. Compensar la ocupación del espacio construido y el espacio libre es uno de los objetivos principales que se persigue. Por otro lado, y para facilitar la orientación dentro del complejo de oficinas se ha hecho especial hincapié en diferenciar cada uno de los patios de los restantes. Ello provoca que se identifiquen los diferentes lugares de trabajo con un patio concreto. Dada la magnitud del proyecto se muestra tan solo una selección de algunos de los patios.

# Patios Gruner+Jahr

### Design: West&Partner, landscape architects

Location: **Hamburg, Germany**

Construction date: **1991**

Photos: © **West&Partner**

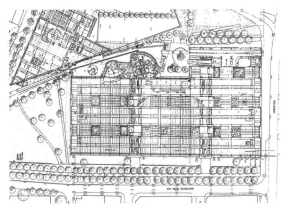

Location plan

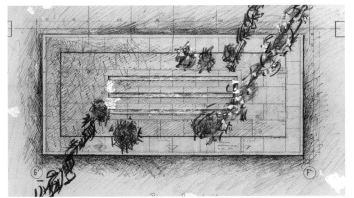

Sketch 1

Sketch 2

The Taylor-Cullity garden is clearly divided into six separate areas, each with its own character and atmosphere, expressed through the use of different colors, textures and forms. In each case the design takes into account not only the underlying concept but also factors such as the gradient and the type of buildings surrounding the space. Movement is the thread that links all these spaces. Permanent sculptures and temporary installations are to be found dotted all over the garden.

Der Garten von Taylor-Cullity ist in sechs Bereiche unterteilt. Jeder davon besitzt einen eigenen Charakter, der durch die Verwendung von verschiedenen Farben, Beschaffenheiten, Formen und Gesten zum Ausdruck kommt. Die Gestaltung berücksichtigt nicht nur das jeweilige Konzept sondern auch Faktoren wie das Gefälle des Geländes und die Bauweise der umliegenden Gebäude. Das Bindeglied zwischen all diesen Räumen ist die Bewegung. Bleibende und vergängliche Skulpturen sind über den Garten verteilt.

Le jardin de Taylor-Cullity présente une compartimentation en six lieux. Chacun a son caractère et son ambiance propres, s'exprimant par l'emploi de différentes couleurs, textures, formes et gestes. Le design de chacun répond non seulement à son propre concept mais tient aussi compte de facteurs comme la pente et la typologie de la construction voisine. Le mouvement est le fil conducteur de tous ces espaces. Sculptures permanentes et éphémères se trouvent réparties dans le jardin.

El jardín de Taylor-Cullity presenta una compartimentación en seis estancias. Cada una tiene un carácter y ambiente propios que se expresan mediante el empleo de diferentes colores, texturas formas y gestos. El diseño de cada uno de ellos responde no sólo al concepto del mismo sino que tiene en cuenta factores como la pendiente y la tipología edificatoria circundante. El movimiento es el hilo conductor de todos estos espacios. Esculturas permanentes y efímeras se encuentran repartidas por el jardín.

# aylor Cullity Residence Garden

Design: Taylor Cullity Lethlean, landscape architect
Sculptures: Kate Cullity and Ryan Sims

Location: **Adelaide, Australia**
Construction date: **2001**
Photos: **© Edward James / Ben Wrigley**

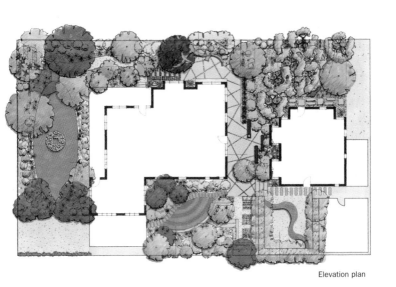

Elevation plan

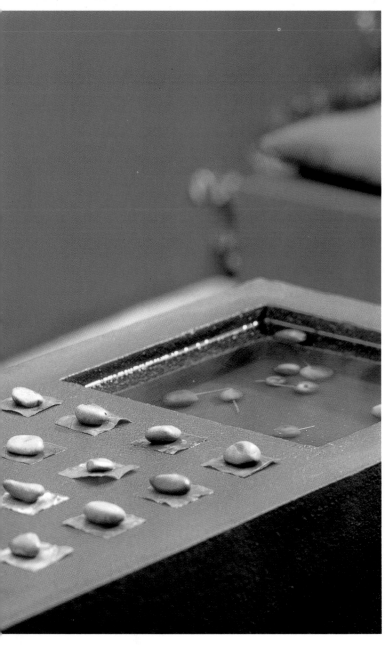

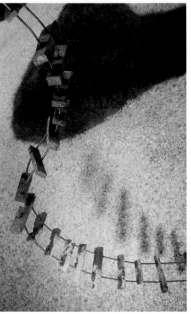

▨ Here the idea was to make a garden that would serve both as a children's play space and a boatshed on a small plot of land (65 x 55 sq. ft.) with extremely uneven terrain and substantial outcrops of rocks. The result was this Garden of Walls, an extremely expressive space conceived with sculptural flourishes. The landscape is dominated by three main elements: the rocky outcrops inherent to the site, the plastered walls painted in warm colors and the vegetation, which embraces *Eucalyptus haemastoma*, *Penissetum alupecuroides*, *Doodia aspera*, *Agave attenuata*, *Liriope muscari*, *Pandorea jasminoides*, *Wisteria sinensis*, *Anigozanthos sp.* and *Phoenix canariensis*.

▨ Der Auftrag bestand in der Gestaltung eines kleineren Geländes (20 x 17 m) mit großen Höhenunterschieden und starken Felsaufwerfungen als Spielplatz für Kinder und mit einem Unterstand für Boote. Das Ergebnis ist dieser Mauergarten, ein Ort mit starker Ausdruckskraft, in dem skulpturale Formen vorherrschen. Er besteht aus drei landschaftlichen Hauptelementen: den örtlich bedingt zutage tretenden Felsformationen, den farbig vergipsten Wänden und der Vegetation, die aus *Eucalyptus haemastoma*, *Penissetum alupecuroides*, *Doodia aspera*, *Agave attenuata*, *Liriope muscari*, *Pandorea jasminoides*, *Wisteria sinensis*, *Anigozanthos sp* und *Phoenix canariensis* besteht.

▨ Concevoir un jardin pouvant offrir un espace de loisirs aux enfants et accueillir une remise à bateaux, telle était la commande reçue pour un terrain de faibles dimensions (20 x 17 m) présentant de forts dénivelés et des affleurements rocheux. Ce jardin des murs en est le résultat, un lieu très expressif où prédomine le langage sculptural. Trois éléments paysagers principaux lui donnent ses formes : les affleurements rocheux propres au lieu, les murs cimentés aux couleurs chaudes et la végétation comprenant *Eucalyptus haemastoma*, *Penissetum alupecuroides*, *Doodia aspera*, *Agave attenuata*, *Liriope muscari*, *Pandorea jasminoides*, *Wisteria sinensis*, *Anigozanthos sp* et *Phoenix canariensis*.

▨ Diseñar un jardín que sirviese de espacio de recreo para niños y que albergara un cobertizo para embarcaciones fue el encargo recibido para un terreno de dimensiones reducidas (20 x 17 m), fuertes desniveles e importantes afloramientos rocosos. El resultado es este jardín de muros, un lugar de gran expresividad en el que predomina el lenguaje escultórico. Tres son los principales elementos paisajísticos que lo conforman; los afloramientos rocosos propios del lugar, los muros enyesados con colores cálidos y la vegetación, compuesta por *Eucalyptus haemastoma*, *Penissetum alupecuroides*, *Doodia aspera*, *Agave attenuata*, *Liriope muscari*, *Pandorea jasminoides*, *Wisteria sinensis*, *Anigozanthos sp* y *Phoenix canariensis*.

# Garden of Walls

**Design: Vladimir Sitta, assistance Maren Parry, Terragram Pty. Ltd., landscape architects**

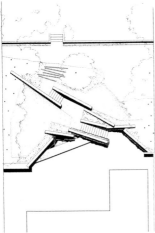

Elevation plan

Location: **Northern Suburbs, Sydney, Australia**

Construction date: **1999**

Photos: © **Walter Glover, Terragram Pty. Ltd.**

By breaking up the pre-existing perceptual limits, the garden refuses to settle with being merely a residual corridor and acquires its own personality. The architectural contructions merge into the forms of the plant world, with the walls and paving seemingly blending into the lawn and the vegetation clipped into sharply defined geometric forms. Pozzi has also created strong color contrasts between the intense green of the grass, the brightness of the *Arenaria indiana* and the white of the walls. The garden's structure is supported by "hardscape" pieces.

Durch das Aufbrechen der vorhandenen Wahrnehmungsgrenzen wird erreicht, dass der Garten nicht nur ein Durchgang in einen Wohnbereich ist, sondern eine ganz eigene Persönlichkeit erhält. Die architektonischen Formen verschwimmen mit denen der Pflanzenwelt. So scheinen sich die Mauern und der Bodenbelag mit dem Rasen zu verschmelzen, während in Form geschnittene pflanzliche Elemente geometrische Formen annehmen. Pozzi hat sich für Lösungen entschieden, welche die chromatischen Kontraste verstärken; das intensive Grün des Rasens, die Leuchtkraft der *Arenaria indiana* und das Weiß der kleinen Mauern. Die Gartenstruktur ruht auf Teilen aus „hardscape".

En réduisant les limites perceptuelles existantes, le jardin loin de se résigner à être un passage résiduel acquiert une personnalité propre. Les images architecturales se diluent avec celle du monde végétal. Ainsi les murs et le sol paraissent se fondre avec la pelouse, alors que la végétation se géométrise par la grâce d'un art topiaire. Pozzi a opté pour les solutions stimulant les contrastes chromatiques : le vert intense du gazon, la luminosité de la *Arenaria indiana* et la blancheur des murets. La structure du jardin repose sur les pièces « hardscape ».

Al desmenuzar los límites perceptuales existentes, el jardín, lejos de resignarse a ser un pasillo residual, adquiere personalidad propia. Las imágenes arquitectónicas se diluyen con las del mundo vegetal. Así, los muros y el pavimento parecen fundirse con el prado, mientras que los elementos vegetales se geometrizan por medio de topiarias. Pozzi ha optado por soluciones que potencian los contrastes cromáticos; el verde intenso del prado, la luminosidad de la *Arenaria indiana* y el blanco de los muretes. La estructura del jardín se apoya sobre piezas "hardscape".

# Casa-Natura Garden
### Design: Patrizia Pozzi, landscape architect

Location: **Carnate, Italy**
Construction date: **1999/2000**
Photos: **© Douglas Andreetti**

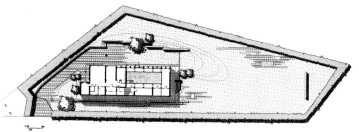

Elevation plan

Isamu Noguchi declared: "An empty space is lacking in any scale, significance and dimension until a line or object is introduced into it". The size, form and placement of each of the sculptures in the garden of the Isamu Noguchi Museum establish close links not only with the other pieces but also with the perimeter wall that shields the garden from its urban surroundings. Each sculpture can be observed from several angles; the visitors' active participation and mobility gives every object on show a central role, and so perception, far from being static, involves continuous movement and change.

Isamu Noguchi sagte: „Ein leerer Raum besitzt solange keinen Maßstab, keine Bedeutung und keine Dimension, bis eine Linie oder ein Objekt einbezogen wird." Größe, Form und Unterteilung aller Skulpturen des Gartens des Isamu Noguchi-Museums stehen in enger Verbindung mit den übrigen Teilen und der umlaufenden Mauer, die den Garten in seinem urbanen Kontext begrenzt. Jede Einzelne der Skulpturen kann aus verschiedenen Blickwinkeln betrachtet werden und dank der Anteilnahme und Beweglichkeit des Besuchers ist es möglich, dass jedes der Elemente als zentral betrachtet wird. So ist die Wahrnehmung bei weitem nicht statisch, sondern befindet sich in ständiger Bewegung und Veränderung.

Comme l'affirmait Isamu Noguchi lui-même : « Un espace vide manque d'échelle, de signifié et de dimension tant qu'une ligne ou un objet ne s'y inscrit pas. » La taille, la forme et la distribution de chacune des pièces sculptées apparaissant dans le jardin du musée de Noguchi entretiennent un lien étroit avec les autres pièces et le mur de périmètre, isolant le jardin du contexte urbain. Chaque sculpture peut être observée sous différents angles et, grâce à l'action participative du visiteur et à sa mobilité, chaque objet exposé peut être considéré comme central. Ainsi, la perception, loin d'être statique, est celle d'un mouvement continu et de changement.

Isamu Noguchi afirmaba: "Un espacio vacío carece de escala, significado y dimensión hasta que no se introduce en él una línea u objeto." El tamaño, la forma y la distribución de cada una de las piezas escultóricas que aparecen en el jardín del Museo de Isamu Noguchi mantienen un estrecho vínculo con las demás piezas y con el muro perimetral que aísla el jardín de su contexto urbano. Cada escultura puede ser observada desde ángulos distintos y gracias a la acción participativa del visitante y su movilidad cada objeto expuesto puede ser considerado central. De esta manera la percepción, lejos de ser estática, es de continuo movimiento y cambio.

# Museumsgarden Isamu Noguchi

### Design: Isamu Noguchi, artist

Location: **New York, USA**
Construction date: **1983**
Photos: **© Mihail Moldoveanu**

The extremely uneven terrain of this plot has been modified by a series of narrow terraces that form the various settings in the garden. The "habitable garden" lies next to the house, seemingly as an extension of the living space, and it can be seen from the bedrooms. Then comes the "bathing garden", which comprises a swimming pool, a lawn and a wooden platform. Higher up, another terrace comprises a relaxation area bounded by plane trees and a pond, both of which were already present before this garden was designed. The other terraces are marked off by hedges and small containing walls. All the newly planted trees are maples (*Acer sp.*) of various origins.

Das schwierige Gelände wurde durch die Anlage schmaler Terrassen verändert, auf denen sich die verschiedenen Bereiche des Gartens befinden. In einem vom Wohnhaus zurückgesetzten Bereich und gerade so, als ob es eine Verlängerung desselben wäre, befindet sich der „Wohngarten", der von allen Zimmer aus zu sehen ist. Im Anschluss erstreckt sich der „Bädergarten" mit dem Swimmingpool, der Wiese und einem Holzpodest. Auf einer weiter oben liegenden Terrasse befindet sich der Aufenthaltsbereich, der von Platanen und einem Teich begrenzt ist, die sich dort befanden. Hecken und kleine Begrenzungsmauern fassen die verschiedenen Terrassen ein. Alle neu gepflanzten Bäume sind verschiedene Ahornarten (*Acer sp.*).

La topographie compliquée de la parcelle a été modifiée par d'étroites terrasses où s'organisent les différentes ambiances du jardin. Dans un recoin de la demeure, et comme en prolongement, se trouve la zone du « jardin habitable », visible depuis les chambres. Vient ensuite le « jardin du bain », comprenant la piscine, la pelouse et un plancher de bois. Une terrasse supérieure accueille une zone de séjour délimitée par des platanes et un bassin, deux éléments préexistants du lieu. Haies et petits murs de contention recueillent les différentes terrasses. Tous les nouveaux arbres sont des érables de diverses provenance (*Acer sp.*).

La complicada topografía de la parcela se modificó a modo de estrechas terrazas donde se organizan los diferentes ambientes del jardín. En un retranqueo de la vivienda y como si fuese una prolongación de la misma, se ubica la zona del "jardín habitable", que queda visible desde las habitaciones. A continuación se encuentra "el jardín del baño", que incorpora la piscina, la pradera y una tarima de madera. En una terraza superior se ubica una zona de estar delimitada por plátanos y una charca, ambos elementos preexistentes en el lugar. Setos y pequeños muros de contención recogen las diferentes terrazas. Todos los árboles nuevos son arces de diferentes procedencias (*Acer sp.*).

# Küsnacht Private Garden

**Design: Raderschall, landscape architect, and Hühnerwadel Albers, architects**

Location: **Küsnacht, Switzerland**
Construction date: **2002**
Photos: © **Giorgio Hoch**

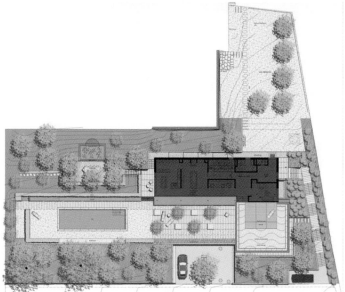

Elevation plan

The number of materials used for the garden has been reduced to the bare minimum: concrete, wood, glass, slate and plants. A concrete wall marks out the boundary of the grounds, as well as keeping them out of view of passersby. A gap in the wall provides access to a patio, which in turn leads on to the house. Opposite the main concrete wall, an enclosure has been erected, consisting of screens with a metal grid covered with plants that contrast with the severe linearity of the wall. All the spaces, including the walls and ceilings both inside and outside the house, are laid out on the basis of modules measuring 52 inches square, produced from a metal mould.

Die Anzahl der bei diesem Garten verwendeten Werkstoffe wurde weitestmöglich gering gehalten: Beton, Holz, Glas, Schiefer und Pflanzen. Eine Betonmauer schafft den Zugang zum Wohngebäude und verschließt es zur Stadt hin. Eine Öffnung in dieser Mauer erschließt durch einen Innenhof den Eingang. Gegenüber der dominierenden Mauer aus Beton wurde eine Begrenzung in Form von bepflanzten Paneelen gestaltet, die auf einer Metallstruktur gelagert sind und deren Anordnung und Komposition mit der Bestimmtheit und klaren Ausrichtung der Mauer kontrastiert. Die Innen- und Außenräume des gesamten Hauses sind nach dem Raster 1,35 x 1,35 m ausgelegt, der durch die Metallverschalung von Mauern und Bindewerk entsteht.

Le nombre des matériaux employés pour le jardin a été limité au minimum : béton, bois, verre, ardoise et végétation. Un mur de béton génère l'accès à la demeure et la ferme sur le centre urbain. Une brèche dans ce mur ouvre l'entrée de la maison à travers un patio. Face au mur principal en béton, une fermeture a été conçue à l'aide de panneaux de végétation flottante sur une structure métallique, dont la disposition et la composition contrastent avec l'emphase et la directionnalité du mur. Les espaces intérieurs et extérieurs de toute la maison sont dimensionnés avec un module de 1,35 x 1,35 m, formé par le coffrage métallique des murs et des éléments forgés.

El número de materiales empleados para el jardín se ha simplificado al máximo: hormigón, madera, vidrio, pizarra y vegetación. Un muro de hormigón genera el acceso a la vivienda y la cierra hacia el casco urbano. Una brecha en este muro abre la entrada de la vivienda a través de un patio. Frente al muro principal de hormigón se ha diseñado un cerramiento a modo de pantallas vegetales flotantes sobre estructura metálica, cuya disposición y composición contrastan con la rotundidad y direccionalidad del muro. Los espacios interiores y exteriores de toda la casa están dimensionados con el módulo de 1,35 x 1,35 m, formado por el encofrado metálico de muros y forjados.

# arden in Santa Margarita

Design: Sánchez-Cantalejo y Tomás, architect, and
Bet Figueras, landscape architect

Location: **Mallorca, Spain**
Construction date: **2001**
Photos: © **Bet Figueras**

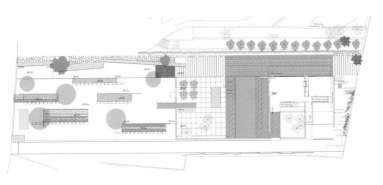

Elevation plan

Armed with a general plan, the client himself set about bringing the project to life on its own. That is why the materials are of an easily manageable size and, in many cases, recycled. The three fields of activity are: the patio/eating area facing the house and backed by the pool, the lush borders around the perimeter and a more intimate central area set off by small trees. These are all linked by a pathway running down the length of the garden and a wooden structure with climbing hydrangeas. The garden is reached from the house by a tiered staircase made of wood and fiberglass, which also doubles as a parking lot for bicycles.

Auf der Grundlage eines Planes übernahm der Kunde selbst die Ausführung der Gartengestaltung. Aus diesem Grund sind die Materialien von geringen Ausmaßen und in vielen Fällen recycelt. Die drei Nutzungsbereiche sind folgende: Innenhof-Essecke in unmittelbarer Nähe des Hauses und des Teichs, umlaufend ein wiesenartiger Bereich und der zentrale, geschütztere Bereich mit Waldvegetation. Sie sind alle durch einen längs verlaufenden Steg und eine Holzstruktur mit Kletterhortensien verbunden. Das Haus und der Garten sind durch eine Kaskadentreppe aus Holz und Glasfaser verbunden, die gleichzeitig als Abstellplatz für Fahrräder dient.

À partir d'un plan général, le client s'est chargé d'exécuter lui-même le projet de jardin. De ce fait, les matériaux sont de dimensions réduites et souvent recyclés. Les trois aires d'activité sont : le patio-salle à manger intégrant la zone jouxtant la maison et l'étang, la zone périphérique de gazon et le centre, plus intimiste, avec une végétation forestière. Chacune est unie aux autres par un chemin longitudinal et une structure de bois aux hortensias grimpantes. La relation maison-jardin s'établit avec un escalier en cascade, en bois et fibre de verre, servant de remise à bicyclette.

A partir de un plan general, el propio cliente se encargó de ejecutar el proyecto del jardín. Por ese motivo los materiales son de pequeñas dimensiones y en muchos casos reciclados. Las tres áreas de actividad son: el patio-comedor que comprende la zona inmediata a la casa y el estanque, la zona perimetral de prado y una zona central más intimista con vegetación forestal. Todas ellas están unidas por una pasera longitudinal y una estructura de madera con hortensias trepadoras. La relación de la casa con el jardín se produce por medio de una escalera en cascada hecha de madera y fibra de vidrio que sirve a la vez de almacén de bicicletas.

# Howland Garden 1

### Design: Plant Architect Inc., landscape architects

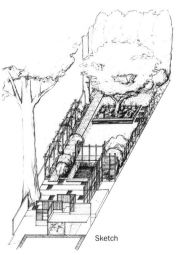

Sketch

Location: **Toronto, Canada**

Construction date: **2002**

Photos: © **Christopher Pommer, Peter Legris**

A mere list of the materials used in this garden indicates its powerful metaphorical content: water, fire, marble, granite, bronze, copper, slate and steel. Fire, a tool exploited by the nomadic Aboriginals to control their lands, reappears in this suburban lot to invoke a time and space beyond the frontiers of the garden itself. A bronze egg on a granite cross simultaneously refers to both pagan and Christian mythologies. Water, and the sound it makes, adds a touch of subdued calm to this highly dramatic setting. The irregular, rough-edged slithers of granite suggest elements of a far bigger scale: mountain ranges, waves, etc.

Schon allein die Aufzählung der für diesen Garten verwendeten Materialarten weist auf den starken metaphorischen Inhalt hin: Wasser, Feuer, Marmor, Granit, Bronze, Kupfer, Schiefer und Stahl. Feuer als Werkzeug, das von den nomadischen Aborigines für die Bodenkontrolle benutzt wurde, taucht in dieser Vorortparzelle erneut auf, als Reminiszenz an über die Grenzen des Gartens selbst hinausreichende, zeitliche und räumliche Dimensionen. Ein Ei aus Bronze auf einem Granitkreuz evoziert gleichzeitig heidnische und christliche Mythologie. Das Wasser und seine Geräusche verleihen diesem hochdramatischen Raum Ruhe und Stille. Die unregelmäßig geformten Granitstreifen spielen auf großformatigere Elemente an: Bergketten, Wellen, usw.

La seule énumération des matériaux employés pour ce jardin donne une indication sur son essence métaphorique : eau, feu, marbre, granite, bronze, cuivre, ardoise et acier. Le feu, un outil avec lequel les aborigènes nomades gèrent leurs terres, réapparaît dans cette parcelle suburbaine, évoquant un temps et un espace allant bien au-delà des frontières mêmes du jardin. Un œuf de bronze sur une croix de granite fait référence à la fois aux mythologies païennes et chrétiennes. L'eau et sa musique apportent la tranquillité dans un contexte très dramatique. Les bandes de granite au profil irrégulier font allusion à des éléments propres d'une autre échelle : chaînes de montagne, vagues, etc.

La sola enumeración de los materiales empleados en este jardín da indicaciones acerca de su fuerte componente metafórico: agua, fuego, mármol, granito, bronce, cobre, pizarra y acero. El fuego, como herramienta con la que los aborígenes nómadas gestionaban sus tierras, reaparece en esta parcela suburbana, invocando a un tiempo y un espacio que van más allá de las fronteras del propio jardín. Un huevo de bronce sobre una cruz de granito hace referencia a la vez a mitologías paganas y cristianas. El agua y su sonido aportan tranquilidad en este contexto de fuerte dramatismo. Las franjas de granito de perfil irregular aluden a elementos propios de otra escala: cadenas montañosas, olas, etcétera.

# Garden of Fire

**Design: Terragram Pty. Ltd., landscape architects**

Location: **Sydney, Australia**

Construction date: **1998**

Photos: **© Walter Glover**

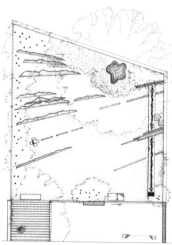

Elevation plan

▨ Jan Bleys based his design on the pre-existing boundaries of the plot, which mark out four different areas, linked by a gravel path. The green area, a classic English meadow bordered by evergreen hedges and set off by a long bench, contrasts with the dynamic forms of the water in the neighboring area, which displays a strong Arab influence. The central space, the amphitheater and the concrete terrace draw on the idea of the Mediterranean patio. The interpretations of these different cultures provide the basis for a multicultural space that reflects the variety of the forms of communication in today's society.

▨ Das Design Jan Bleys basiert auf den bereits bestehenden Begrenzungen des Grundstücks, durch die vier unterschiedliche Bereiche vorgegeben sind. Die Grünzone, ein klassischer englischer Rasen mit durchgehender Bank, der von immergrünen Sträuchern umgeben ist, kontrastiert mit den dynamischen Formen des Wassers im angrenzenden arabisch beeinflussten Bereich. Im zentralen Bereich geben das Amphitheater und die Betonterrasse den Gedanken eines mediterranen Innenhofs wieder. Alle diese Einzelkomponenten sind durch einen Bodenbelag aus Kies miteinander verbunden. Die Interpretationen dieser unterschiedlichen Kulturen bieten Raum für einen multikulturellen Raum mit Bezug auf die vielfältigen Kommunikationsformen unserer modernen Gesellschaft.

▨ Jan Bleys fonde son design sur les limites préexistantes de la parcelle, déterminant quatre secteurs différents. La partie verte, un pré anglais classique avec un banc continu et entouré d'arbustes persistants, contraste avec la présence des formes dynamiques de l'eau dans la zone contiguë, d'influence arabe. L'espace central, l'amphithéâtre et la terrasse de béton reflètent l'idée du patio méditerranéen. Tous les éléments individuels sont unis à l'aide d'un parterre de gravier. Les interprétations de ces différentes cultures invitent à créer un espace multiculturel se référant à la variété des formes de communication de notre société contemporaine.

▨ Jan Bleys basa su diseño en los límites preexistentes de la parcela que determinan cuatro áreas diferentes. La zona verde, un clásico prado inglés con un banco corrido y rodeada de setos perennes, contrasta con la presencia de las formas dinámicas del agua en la zona contigua, de influencia árabe. El espacio central, el anfiteatro y la terraza de hormigón reflejan la idea del patio mediterráneo. Todos los elementos individuales están unidos por medio de un pavimento de grava. Las interpretaciones de estas diferentes culturas invitan a crear un espacio multicultural que refiere a la variedad de formas de comunicación de nuestra sociedad actual.

# Project Tobback

## Design: Jan Bleys, landscape architect

Location: **Aartselaar, Belgium**

Construction date: **2000**

Photos: © **Nicolas Maeterlinck**

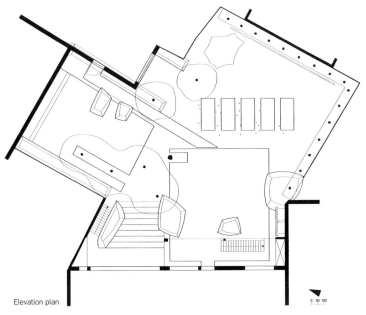

Elevation plan

▦ Here yew hedges are the most characteristic markers of space, evoking the formal divisions of Baroque gardens. The pre-existing conifers were pruned back to allow more light to enter. The terrace, with its basalt paving, leads on to an extensive lawn lined with flower beds and dotted with azaleas and large steel tubs, seemingly scattered at random. These contain seasonal ornamental plants and eye-catching lights. Away from the large main space, *Amelanchier sp.* shrubs define the secondary areas. Their sinuous elegance, white blossoms and orange-toned autumnal foliage contrast with the unbroken linearity of the hedges.

▦ Wie im Parkett eines Barockgartens definieren Eibenhecken den repräsentativsten Bereich. Die vorhandenen Koniferen wurden so beschnitten, dass man durch sie hindurch sehen kann. Von der Terrasse mit Basaltboden ist die ausgedehnte Rasenfläche mit Blumenbeeten und Azaleenpflanzungen zu sehen. Große Stahlkübel sind scheinbar willkürlich zwischen den Bäumen verteilt. Die je nach Saison blühenden Zierpflanzen und die Beleuchtungselemente in ihrem Inneren machen sie zu deutlichen Bezugspunkten. Außerhalb der großen Hauptfläche bestimmten *Amelanchier sp.*-Sträucher die sekundären Bereiche. Ihre Form, die weißen Blüten und ihr orangefarbenes Herbstlaub stehen im Kontrast zur strengen Geometrie der Eiben.

▦ Comme sur un parquet de jardin baroque, des haies d'ifs définissent l'espace le plus représentatif. Les conifères existants sont soumis à un élagage de transparence. Depuis la terrasse pavée de basalte se contemple la grande superficie de gazon aux parterres de fleurs et aux plantations d'azalées. De grands conteneurs d'acier sont répartis de manière apparemment aléatoire parmi les arbres. À l'intérieur, des plantes ornementales de saison et des éléments d'éclairage les convertissent en foyers d'attraction. Hors de la grande superficie principale, les arbustes d'*Amelanchier sp.* définissent les espaces secondaires. Aspect, blanche floraison et feuillage automnal orangé contrastent avec la stricte géométrie des haies.

▦ Como en un parquet de jardín barroco, setos de tejos definen el espacio más representativo. Las coníferas existentes son sometidas a una poda de transparencia. Desde la terraza de pavimento de basalto se ve la gran superficie de césped con parterres de flores y plantaciones de azaleas. Hay grandes contenedores de acero repartidos de forma aparentemente aleatoria entre el arbolado. En su interior, plantas de temporada y elementos de iluminación los convierten en claros focos de atracción. Fuera de la superficie principal, arbustos *Amelanchier sp.* definen los espacios secundarios. Su porte, su floración blanca y su foliación otoñal anaranjada contrastan con la geometría de los tejos.

# Fleurop's Garden
### Design: Levin Monsigny, landscape architects

Location: **Berlin, Germany**
Construction date: **1999**
Photos: **© Claas Dreppenstedt / Levin Monsigny**

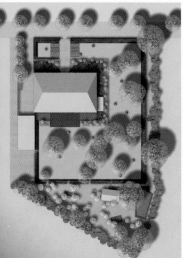

Elevation plan (day view)

Elevation plan (night view)

■ The basis of this design is a unifying treatment of the perimeter of the garden, involving a repetitive, linear pattern of beds with bulbs, shrubs, trees, trellises, benches and paving stones. The various rows alternate and overlap to create several highly distinctive spaces. The sides overlooking the street offer an extrovert display, while the two more intimate areas are tucked against the sides of the house. These spaces are designed according to their function: one is the eating area, covered partly by the branches of trees and partly by a semi-transparent roof; the other is the vegetable garden, set off by evergreens, where the exposure to sunlight is more prolonged.

■ Ausgangspunkt für diesen Garten ist eine einheitliche Einfassung. Sie besteht aus der Wiederholung eines linearen Musters von Beeten mit Zwiebelgewächsen, Büschen, Baumpflanzungen, Spalieren, Bänken und Bodenbelägen. Die verschiedenen Streifen wechseln sich ab und überlagern sich, wodurch sie unterschiedliche Räume schaffen. Die Seitenbereiche auf Straßenhöhe sind einsehbar, während die beiden geschützteren Aufenthaltsbereiche (je nach Nutzungsart unterschiedlich) zu beiden Seiten des Hauses angeordnet sind. Einer davon dient als Essbereich und ist teils durch die Baumkronen, teils durch ein halbtransparentes Dach überdeckt. Der andere Bereich, an dem die Sonneneinstrahlung stärker ist, besteht aus Obst- und Gemüsegärten und immergrüner Vegetation.

■ La proposition part d'un traitement unitaire du périmètre du jardin. Il naît de la répétition d'un plan linéaire de parterres de bulbeuses, d'arbustes, d'arbres, d'espaliers, de bancs et de revêtement. Les diverses franges alternent et se superposent, créant des espaces différenciés. Les flancs, en contact avec la rue, fonctionnent comme une exposition, alors que les deux aires de séjour, plus intimes (différenciées par leur usage) s'organisent autour de chaque côté de la maison. L'une est le coin repas, couverte en partie par la cime des arbres et par une toiture semi transparente ; l'autre correspond au potager et à la végétation pérenne, plus exposée au soleil.

■ La propuesta parte de un tratamiento unitario del perímetro del jardín. Ello se consigue con la repetición de un patrón lineal de parterres de bulbosas, elementos arbustivos, arbolado, espalderas, bancos y pavimentación. Las diferentes franjas se alternan y superponen creando espacios diferenciados. Los laterales en contacto con la calle funcionan a modo de exposición, mientras que las dos zonas de estar más íntimas (diferenciadas según el uso) se organizan a ambos lados de la casa. Una es la zona de comedor, cubierta en parte por las copas de los arboles y en parte por una cubierta semitransparente; la otra es la zona de huertos y vegetación perenne donde la exposición solar es mayor.

# Prince George Drive

**Design: Plant Architect Inc., landscape architects**

Location: **Toronto, Canada**
Construction date: **1999**
Photos: © **Peter Legris, Christopher Pommer**

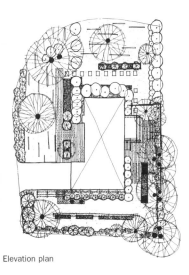

Elevation plan

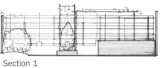

Section 1

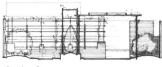

Section 2

The design of this garden draws on the Biblical concept of the Garden of Eden. Fountains, enclosed spaces and fragrances are the main themes of the composition. The garden is organized around three terraces. The first is dominated by a fountain intertwined within a chestnut tree. The second features three fountains immersed in lush vegetation (*Musa basjoo*, *Catalpa*, *Fatsia japonica*, *Fuchsia magellanica*). The third comprises a kitchen garden with traditional vegetables. This garden was once a kind of showcase, where designers could try out different combinations of plants, cultivate particular species and experiment with a diversity of materials.

Das Konzept dieses Gartens ist mit der biblischen Vorstellung des Garten Eden verknüpft. Brunnen, abgeschlossene Räume, Gerüche und Düfte sind die kompositorischen Hauptmotive. Die erste der drei Terrassen des Gartens beherbergt eine von einer verschlungenen Kastanie umgebene Quelle. Auf der zweiten befinden sich drei von üppiger Vegetation umgebene Springbrunnen (*Musa basjoo*, *Catalpa*, *Fatsia japonica*, *Fuchsia magellanica*). Auf der dritten Terrasse erstreckt sich ein Garten mit ursprünglichen Pflanzenarten. Bei der Anlage des Gartens dachten die Gestalter zunächst an einen „Showroom", in welchem sie verschiedene Kombinationen von Pflanzenarten anordneten, ursprüngliche Pflanzensorten pflanzten und mit unterschiedlichen Baumaterialien experimentierten.

Le concept de ce jardin est lié au thème biblique du jardin de l'Eden. Fontaines, espaces clos, saveurs et parfums sont les principaux motifs de la composition. La première des trois terrasses l'organisant est composée d'une fontaine entourée d'un marronnier entrelacé. La deuxième terrasse intègre deux fontaines immergées dans une végétation exubérante (*Musa basjoo*, *Catalpa*, *Fatsia japonica*, *Fuchsia magellanica*). La troisième est occupée par un potager d'espèces végétales primaires. Le jardin put jouer à l'occasion les « show-room », le responsables du projet mettant à l'épreuve diverses associations de plantes, plantant des espèces primaires et expérimentant avec différents matériaux.

El concepto de este jardín está ligado al tema bíblico del jardín del edén. Fuentes, espacios cerrados, sabores y perfumes son los principales motivos de la composición. La primera de las tres terrazas que lo organizan está compuesta por una fuente rodeada por un castaño entrelazado. La segunda terraza incopora tres fuentes inmersas en una vegetación exuberante (*Musa basjoo*, *Catalpa*, *Fatsia japonica*, *Fuchsia magellanica*). La tercera terraza está ocupada por un huerto con especies vegetales primitivas. El jardín tuvo en su día vocación de "show-room", en él los proyectistas pusieron a prueba distintas asociaciones de plantas, plantaron especies primitivas y experimentaron con diferentes materiales.

# The Garden of Paradise

**Design: Arnaud Maurières and Eric Ossart, gardeners**

Location: **Cordes-sur-ciel, France**
Construction date: **1997**
Photos: **© Le Scanff-Mayer**

The Van Egeraat Garden is a small city garden situated in front of an architecture studio in the center of Rotterdam. A path made of polished concrete runs through an expanse of crushed basalt. The lighting elements embedded in the pieces of concrete mark the entrance to the office. The garden contains what is known as the "smallest wood in Holland": a grove of small birches set in an area made up of overlapping pieces of slate. The concrete border around the slate area also has lights built into it.

Der Van Egeraat-Garten ist ein kleiner städtischer Garten, der sich vor einem Architekturbüro im Zentrum Rotterdams befindet. Auf einer Fläche aus Basaltsplitt verläuft in der Art eines Steges ein Pfad aus poliertem Beton. In die Betonteile eingelassene Beleuchtungselemente weisen den Weg zum Büro. Der Garten enthält den sogenannten „kleinsten Wald Hollands", eine Gruppe kleiner Birken auf einer Fläche von übereinander liegenden Schiefertafeln. In der Betonumfassung derselben sind ebenfalls kleine Lampen eingelassen.

Van Egeraat Garden est un petit jardin urbain situé devant une étude d'architecture au centre de Rotterdam. Sur une surface en basalte concassé passe, comme un sentier, une allée de béton lustré. Les éléments d'éclairage sertis dans les pièces de bétons indiquent l'entrée du bureau. Le jardin incorpore ce qui a été nommé le « plus petit bois d´Hollande », un ensemble de petits bouleaux situés sur une surface formée de pièces d'ardoise superposées. La bordure de béton ceignant le parterre d'ardoise comprend également des éclairages intégrés.

Van Egeraat Garden es un pequeño jardín urbano situado delante de un estudio de arquitectura en el centro de Rotterdam. Sobre una superficie de basalto machacado transcurre, a modo de pasera, un sendero de hormigón pulido. Los elementos de iluminación que se encuentran incrustados en las piezas de hormigón indican la entrada a la oficina. El jardín incorpora el que se denomina "bosque más pequeño de Holanda"; un conjunto de pequeños abedules ubicados en una superficie formada por piezas de pizarra superpuestas entre sí. El bordillo de hormigón que rodea la superficie de pizarras incorpora también luminarias incrustadas.

# Van Egeraat Garden

### Design: Adriaan Geuze, landscape architect

Location: **Rotterdam, Netherlands**
Construction date: **1994**
Photos: © **Jeroen Musch / West 8**

This garden, stretching over only 5,000 sq. ft., is an example of a quiet, intimate space in an urban setting. The choice of plants is intended to provide several blooms throughout the year: narcissi and lilies in spring, dahlias and Japanese anemones in summer. Higher up, the *Fraxinus ornus* tree spreads out like a sunshade and provides protection from the wind. The rubber flooring, which absorbs the sound of footsteps, and the sprinklers, which ensure a high level of humidity, make this garden an ideal spot for relaxing. The glossy acrylic lamps slowly emit the light that has been stored up during the day, thereby creating patterns of light that vary as the night goes on.

Dieser Garten ist nur 500 m² groß und Beispiel für einen stillen und abgeschiedenen Ort inmitten urbaner Umgebung. Die Blütezeiten der verschiedenen Pflanzen wechseln sich ab. Im Frühling Narzissen und Lilien, im Sommer Dalien und japanische Anemonen. Im Baumbestand bietet der schattenspendenden *Fraxinus ornus* windgeschützte Räume. Das ärmschluckende Kautschukpflaster und ein hohes Maße an Feuchtigkeit garantierende Sprinkleranlagen unterstützen die angenehme Atmosphäre im ganzen Komplex. Die Lampen aus satiniertem Acryl geben langsam das während des Tages gespeicherte Licht ab und schaffen so im Verlauf der Nacht unterschiedliche Lichtatmosphären.

Ce jardin de seulement 500 m² est un exemple d'espace silencieux et intimiste dans un cadre urbain. Les plantes permettent de profiter des diverses floraisons au long de l'année : narcisses et iris au printemps, dahlias et anémones japonaises en été. Dans le stratum boisé, le *Fraxinus ornus*, avec son chapeau, crée des espaces parcourus par le vent. Le revêtement en gomme absorbant le son des pas et les vaporisateurs maintenant un haut niveau d'humidité aident à convertir l'ensemble en un lieu à l'atmosphère agréable. Les luminaires en acrylique satiné libèrent lentement la lumière emmagasinée le jour, créant diverses situations d'éclairage tout au long de la nuit.

Este jardín de tan solo 500 m² es un ejemplo de espacio silencioso e intimista en un entorno urbano. Las plantas permiten disfrutar de diferentes floraciones a lo largo del año: narcisos y lirios en primavera, dalias y anémonas japonesas en verano. En el estrato arbóreo el *Fraxinus ornus*, con su porte de sombrilla, crea espacios recogidos del viento. El pavimento de caucho que absorbe el sonido de las pisadas y los vaporizadores que mantienen un elevado grado de humedad ayudan a convertir el conjunto en un lugar de ambiente agradable. Las luminarias de acrílico satinado desprenden lentamente la luz almacenada durante el día, creando diferentes situaciones lumínicas a lo largo de la noche.

# Columbinehave in Tivoli
Design: Stig L. Andersson and Stine Poulsen, landscape architects

Location: **Copenhagen, Denmark**

Construction date: **2001**

Photos: © **Jens Lindhe, Stig L. Andersson**

Elevation plan

243

This garden, based on a pavilion inspired by the traditions of Andalusia, is divided into two spaces: a gravel-covered patio, adorned with flower pots, that leads on to the original building, and a paved area at the foot of the pavilion. Various smaller areas, separated by small paths, are incorporated into these two larger spaces. For example, one contains a swimming pool and three ponds, one of these with aquatic plants; another boasts an apricot tree planted in a patch of grass; a third is occupied by some oaks that predate this design, along with a collection of exotic plants and sculptures by Odile Rosso, while a fourth has more oaks, complemented by a bed of brightly colored geraniums.

Auf der Grundlage eines von der andalusischen Tradition inspirierten Pavillons ist der Garten in zwei Bereiche unterteilt: ein Innenhof mit Kiesbelag der zum ursprünglichen Gebäude führt in dem sich Pflanzenkübel befinden und ein gepflasterter Raum am Fuße des Pavillons. Diese beiden Bereiche sind von mehreren, durch kleine Pfade getrennte Räume überlagert. In einem befinden sich zwei Teiche, ein Swimmingpool und ein Teich mit Wasserpflanzen. In einem anderen erhebt sich ein Aprikosenbaum über grasbewachsenem Boden. Ein dritter Bereich beherbergt alte Eichen, eine Sammlung exotischer Pflanzen und Skulpturen von Odile Rosso. Der letzte schließlich besteht aus Eichen und einem Teppich von stark farbigen Geranien.

À partir de la construction d'un pavillon inspiré de la tradition andalouse, le projet de jardin se divise en deux espaces : un patio de gravier qui se livre à l'immeuble d'origine et occupé par des pots, et un espace dallé au pied du pavillon. Superposées à ces deux espaces, s'organisent différntes zones séparées par de petits sentiers. L'une incorpore deux plans d'eau, une piscine et un étang de plantes aquatiques ; une autre est occupée par un abricotier sur un parterre d'herbe ; une troisième prend forme grâce à des chênes préexistants, une collection de plantes exotiques et des sculptures d'Odile Rosso. La dernière comprend des chênes et un tapis de géraniums vivaces.

A partir de la construcción de un pabellón inspirado en la tradición andalusí, el proyecto del jardín está dividido en dos espacios; un patio de gravilla que se entrega al edificio original y que está ocupado por macetas y un espacio pavimentado al pie del pavellón. Superpuestos a estos dos espacios se organizan diferentes zonas separadas por pequeños senderos. Una incorpora dos estanques, una piscina y un estanque de plantas acuáticas; otra zona la ocupa un albaricoquero sobre un parterre de hierba; un tercer espacio otra lo conforman unos robles preexistentes, una colección de plantas exóticas y esculturas de Odile Rosso, y el último está compuesto por robles y un tapiz de geranios vivaces.

# Fournials' Garden
### Design: Arnaud Maurières and Eric Ossart, gardeners

Location: **Albi-Rodez, France**
Construction date: **1994**
Photos: **© Le Scanff-Mayer**

The paving in the center of this garden serves to distribute the space, while an Italian ramp connects the patio with the street level. The red wall marking off the patio space and separating it from the living space has an open strip running across the top, thereby establishing a relationship between the interior and the exterior. The concrete wall retains the marks of the plank molds, endowing it with an almost stony appearance. Water also plays a part, with a long, thin pool setting up an interplay of reflections and a waterfall sending reverberations throughout the space. The use of *Prunus sargentii* adds the final poetic touch.

Die Fläche aus Pflastersteinen im Zentrum dieses Gartens dient als verteilendes Element und eine italienische Rampe schafft den Übergang zwischen der Straßenebene und der des Innenhofs. Die rote Mauer, welche den Innenhof räumlich begrenzt und von der Straße trennt, enthält einen längs verlaufenden Schlitz, der eine Verbindung zwischen innen und außen schafft. Die Betonmauer zeigt die Spuren der Verschalungshölzer, was ihr ein nahezu steinartiges Aussehen gibt. Wie ein Film gleitet das Wasser abwärts und spielt mit den enstehenden Reflektionen. Das Geräusch des Wasserfalls rundet das Stimmungsbild der Anlage ab. Die Bepflanzung mit *Prunus sargentii* fügt den letzten poetischen Pinselstrich hinzu.

La superficie goudronnée du centre de ce jardin exerce une fonction distributrice et une rampe à l'italienne lie la hauteur de la rue et celle du patio. Le mur rouge délimitant le patio et le séparant de l'espace de passage incorpore une ouverture longitudinale établissant une relation intérieur/extérieur. Le mur de béton conserve les marques des bois de coffrage lui conférant une apparence quasi pétrifiée. L'eau apparaît comme une feuille qui permet de jouer avec le reflet créé et, en cascade, elle apporte le son à l'ensemble. La présence de *Prunus sargentii* donne l'ultime touche poétique.

La superficie adoquinada en el centro de este jardín ejerce de elemento distribuidor y una rampa italiana enlaza la altura de la calle con la del patio. El muro rojo que delimita el patio incorpora una abertura longitudinal que permite establecer una relación entre interior y exterior. El muro de hormigón conserva las marcas de las maderas de encofrado que le dan una apariencia casi pétrea. El agua aparece como una lámina que permite jugar con el reflejo que genera, y la cascada aporta sonido al conjunto. La presencia de *Prunus sargentii* acaba de darle la última pincelada poética.

# Laboratoriumstreet

**Design: Rotzler Krebs Partner, landscape architects**

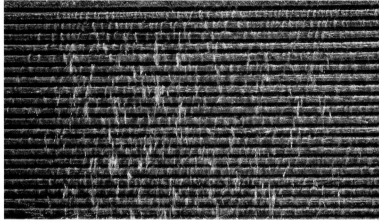

Location: **Wintherthur, Switzerland**
Construction date: **1999**
Photos: © **Gaston Wicky**

Section 1                                    Section 2

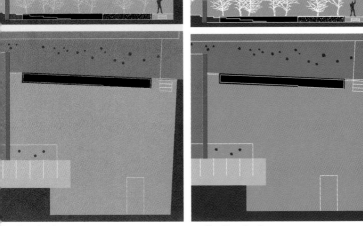

Elevation plan 1                             Elevation plan 2

This garden is comprised of three main elements: wrought iron, wooden trellises and rough-hewn stone paths. The layout is determined by the intensity of the light in each space. Every area is marked off by metal and wood latticework with deciduous creepers, which ensure more visibility in winter. The eating area is set inside a wrought-iron enclosure adorned with climbing vine. The sculpture garden—the shadiest area—contains a long bench, perfectly placed for contemplating the pieces of sculpture lodged in the gravel. The reading area receives the most sunlight. A stone path links the house with these three spaces.

Dieser Garten besteht im Wesentlichen aus drei Elementen: Schmiedeeisen, Spaliere aus Holz und Wege aus Naturstein. Die räumliche Aufteilung der Bereiche erschließt sich durch unterschiedliche Beleuchtung. Sie sind durch Gitter aus Metall und Holz mit laubabwerfenden Kletterpflanzen begrenzt, die im Winter mehr Durchsicht erlauben. Der Essbereich befindet sich in einer kastenförmigen Struktur aus Schmiedeeisen und Weinlaub. Der Skulpturengarten als schattigster Bereich besteht aus einer durchgehenden Bank, Kiesboden und Skulpturenpodesten. Der Lesebereich ist der Hellste. Ein Steinweg verbindet das Haus mit diesen drei Zonen.

Trois éléments principaux donnent vie au jardin : fer forgé, espalier de bois et sentier en pierre naturelle. L'organisation des différents espaces s'explique à partir des différentes situations lumineuses. Tous sont délimités par des jalousies en métal et en bois avec des plantes grimpantes caduques offrant une meilleure visibilité en hiver. L'aire de repas est située dans une cage de fer forgé et de vigne vierge. Le jardin des sculptures, la partie la plus sombre, est formé par un banc continu, une surface en gravier et le piédestal des sculptures. La zone de lecture est l'espace le plus lumineux. Un chemin de pierre relie la maison aux trois espaces.

Tres son los elementos principales que configuran este jardín: hierro forjado, espalderas de madera y senderos de piedra natural. La organización de los diferentes espacios se explica a partir de las diferentes situaciones lumínicas. Todos ellos están delimitados por celosías de metal y madera con trepadoras caducas que permiten una mayor visibilidad en invierno. La zona de comedor se encuentra ubicada dentro de una caja de hierro forjado y parra virgen. El jardín de las esculturas, la zona más sombría, la conforman un banco corrido, pavimento de grava y los pedestales de esculturas. La zona de lectura representa el espacio más luminoso. Un camino de piedra vincula la casa con los tres espacios.

# Howland Garden 2
### Design: Plant Architect Inc., landscape architects

Location: **Toronto, Canada**
Construction date: **2002**
Photos: © **Peter Legris, Christopher Pommer**

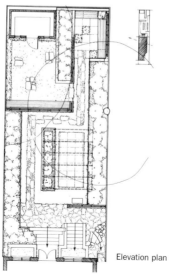

Elevation plan

The premise for this garden was an outward extension of the living space. This concept, and the elongated shape of the plot, has led to the garden's division into several sharply differentiated areas: a sunken central section on the same level as the bedrooms, complete with a pool containing a half-submerged bench; raised side terraces, reveling in exuberant vegetation; and two other more extensive areas, largely given over to unkempt lawns. All the different areas and levels are linked to each other by a straight wooden walkway.

Der Garten, verstanden als Teil des sich nach außen forsetzenden Wohnraums, ist Ausgangspunkt dieses Entwurfs. Dieser Grundgedanke zusammen mit der länglichen Form des Grundstücks münden in eine Untergliederung des Gartens in verschiedene, klar abgegrenzte Bereiche: der mittlere, bis auf die Höhe der Schlafzimmer abgesenkte Bereich, in dem sich ein Teich mit einer zur Hälfte im Wasser liegenden Bank befindet und die seitlichen terrassenförmig angelegten und bewachsenen Ebenen. Hinzu kommen zwei ausgedehnte Bereiche, in denen Wiesen vorherrschen. Sie alle sind durch einen, in Längsrichtung verlaufenden Holzsteg verbunden, der als Bindeglied die Höhenunterschiede überbrückt.

Le jardin, compris comme une partie de l'espace habitable se prolongeant vers l'extérieur, est le point de départ de la proposition. De cette réflexion et de la forme allongée du terrain a résulté une division du jardin en diverses zones clairement différenciées : une zone centrale, cachée jusqu'au niveau des chambres, où se situe un étang avec un banc à demi immergé, les terrasses latérales en plates-formes occupées par la végétation et deux autres parties, plus étendues, où prédomine la pelouse. Toutes les zones sont liées entre elles par une passerelle de bois, au tracé longitudinal, permettant de franchir les dénivelés.

El jardín, entendido como una parte del espacio habitable que se prolonga hacia el exterior, es el punto de partida de esta propuesta. Esa reflexión y la forma alargada de la parcela dan como resultado una división del jardín en varias zonas claramente diferenciadas: una zona central hundida hasta la cota de los dormitorios, en la que se ubica un estanque con un banco semi-sumergido, los aterrazamientos laterales a modo de plataformas ocupadas por vegetación y otras dos zonas más extensivas en las que predomina la superficie de prado. Todas las zonas quedan relacionadas entre sí mediante una pasarela de madera, de trazado longitudinal, que permite superar la diferencia de nivel.

# Garden R.

**Design: 3:0 Landschaftsarchitektur, Gachowetz, Lutz, Zimmermann,
landscape architects**

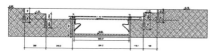

Section of the pool

Elevation plan

Location: **Salzburg, Austria**

Construction date: **2000**

Photos: © **3:0 Landschaftsarchitektur**

This small private garden tackles the problem of limited space without renouncing playfulness and sensuality. The layout imposes a strict demarcation of the different materials (granite, gravel, pebbles and wood) and vegetation (*Ophiopogon japonicus*, miniature *Ophiopogon japonicus*, *Phyllostachys heteroclytaforma*, etc.). The designers have found room for a small swimming pool, a vegetable patch, a belvedere, a terrace and a pergola. Visitors are first greeted by a bougainvillea that twines around a vertical structure, which seemingly takes on the appearance of a tree. The result is a garden which uses a geometric idiom to alternate various textures and colors.

Dieser kleine Privatgarten löst das Problem räumlicher Knappheit, ohne dabei die Suche nach spielerischen und sinnlichen Erfahrungen zu vernachlässigen. Er setzt auf eine strenge Materialordnung (Granit, Split, Kies und Holz) und Bepflanzung (*Ophiopogon japonicus*, *Ophiopogon japonicus* kleine Variante, *Phyllostachys heteroclytaforma*, usw.). Es sind Bereiche für ein kleines Schwimmbecken, einen Obst- und Gemüsegarten, einen Aussichtspunkt, eine Terrasse und eine Pergola vorgesehen. Am Eingang rankt sich als Willkommensgruß eine Bougainvilla um eine senkrechte Struktur, sodass sie wie ein Baum erscheint. Das Ergebnis ist ein Garten mit Betonung der Geometrie, in dem sich verschiedene Oberflächen und Farben abwechseln.

Ce petit jardin particulier répond à un manque d'espace sans pour autant renoncer à la quête d'expériences ludiques et sensorielles. Le défi visait à ordonner strictement les matériaux (granite, graviers, pierres polies et bois) et la végétation (*Ophiopogon japonicus*, *Ophiopogon japonicus* var. naine, *Phyllostachys heteroclytaforma*, etc.). La zonification incorpore une petite piscine, un potager, un mirador, une terrasse et une pergola. Dans l'entrée, en lieu de réception, une bougainvillée s'enroule autour d'une structure verticale lui donnant un air arboricole. Il en résulte un jardin au langage géométrique où alternent différentes textures et couleurs.

Este pequeño jardín particular da respuesta a un problema de falta de espacio sin renunciar a la búsqueda de experiencias lúdicas y sensoriales. La apuesta consiste en una estricta ordenación de materiales (granito, grava, cantos rodados y madera) y vegetación (*Ophiopogon japonicus*, *Ophiopogon japonicus* var. pequeña, *Phyllostachys heteroclytaforma*, etc.). La zonificación incorpora una pequeña piscina, una zona de huerto, un mirador, una terraza y una pérgola. En la entrada y a modo de recepción, una buganvilla se enreda en torno a una estructura vertical que le da un porte arbóreo. El resultado es un jardín de lenguaje geométrico en el que se alternan diferentes texturas y colores.

# Grillo Garden

### Design: Orlando Busarello, Dilva Cândida and Daniela Slomp Busarello, architects

Location: **Curitiba, Brasil**
Construction date: **1999**
Photos: © **Busarello**

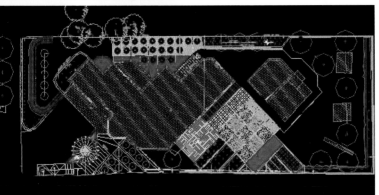

An expanse of wooden planks running parallel to the facade of this family home is the most prominent feature in this 2,600 sq. ft. garden. Some of the planks are cut short to make room for flowerbeds, lawn areas, palm trees in small pits, birches and climbing plants, all laid out in alternating strips to create a striking rhythmic pattern. A continuous bench made of Travertine marble runs lengthwise across the garden. This element not only serves as a seat but also a bar that can be used as an eating surface. Finally, a pergola protects the building's glass façade from direct exposure to the sun.

Eine einheitliche Fläche aus parallel zur Fassade dieses Einfamilienhauses verlaufenden Holzbalken ist das charakteristische Merkmal dieses 240 m² großen Gartens. Einige Balken sind ausgespart und geben Raum frei für Blumenbeete, Rasen und Pflanzgruben für Palmen, Birken und Kletterpflanzen. Das Abwechseln der verschiedenen Streifen verleiht dem Gesamtwerk einen starken Rhythmus. Eine durchgehende Bank aus Travertinmarmor durchquert den Garten in Längsrichtung. Dieses Element dient als Sitzmöglichkeit und als Untergrund für einen Esstisch. Abschließend schützt eine Pergola die Glasfassade des Gebäudes vor direkter Sonneneinstrahlung.

Une superficie unique de planches de bois, parallèle à la façade de la maison familiale, caractérise ce jardin de 240 m². Certaines disparaissent laissant un espace de parterres de plantes fleuries et de gazon et des fosses de palmiers, de bouleaux et de plantes grimpantes. L'alternance des différentes bandes confère un rythme élevé à l'ensemble. Un banc continu en travertine traverse le jardin dans sa longueur. Cet élément sert de siège mais aussi de support sur lequel dresser la table. Enfin, une pergola protège la façade vitrée de l'édifice de l'entrée directe du soleil.

Una única superficie de láminas de madera paralelas a la fachada de la vivienda unifamiliar son el rasgo característico de este jardín de 240 m². Algunas de ellas desaparecen dejando espacio a parterres de plantas de flor y césped y alcorques de palmeras, abedules y plantas trepadoras. La alternancia de las diferentes franjas otorga un fuerte ritmo al conjunto. Un banco corrido de mármol travertino atraviesa el jardín longitudinalmente. Este elemento sirve de asiento, así como de barra sobre la que disponer la mesa. Por último, una pérgola protege la fachada acristalada del edificio de la entrada directa del sol.

# House Monrás

**Design: Various architects**

Location: **Sabadell, Spain**
Construction date: **1994**
Photos: © **Mihail Moldoveanu**

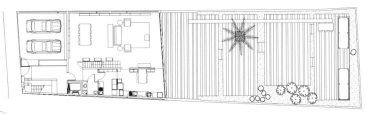

Elevation plan

This garden is intended to combine a leisure area, a vegetable patch and a continuation of the closed living space. Its modest dimensions and linear configuration made subdivision the obvious option for the layout. The resulting subsections merge into each other, creating a mosaic of distinctive fragments with varying uses and plant species. The striped garden in front of the living room comprises a series of aligned beds with alternating varieties of ornamental plants, while the vegetable patch faces the kitchen. To round off, a hedge marks the corner of the garden. The diversity is further heightened by the variations induced by the changing of the seasons.

Dieser Garten wurde als Ort der Entspannung, Obst- und Gemüsegarten sowie als Verlängerung des geschlossenen Wohnraums konzipiert. Seine langgestreckte Form bei geringen Ausmaßen führten zu dieser logischen Unterteilung und Anordnung. Die Untergliederungen überlappen sich, wechseln sich ab und schaffen ein Mosaik aus Teilstücken mit unterschiedlichen Merkmalen, Nutzungsmöglichkeiten und Pflanzenarten. Der streifenförmige Garten vor dem Wohnzimmer ist ein Teppich aus länglichen Beeten, in denen sich verschiedene Arten von Zierpflanzen abwechseln. Vor der Küche befindet sich der Obst- und Gemüsegarten und den Abschluss bildet schließlich eine Hecke in der Ecke des Gartens. Diese Vielfalt wird durch die Veränderung des Gartens im Lauf des Jahres noch verstärkt.

Ce jardin a été pensé comme lieu de loisirs, potager et comme une prolongation de l'espace habitable intérieur. Sa linéarité et ses dimensions réduites font de l'option de la subdivision une solution logique d'organisation. Les sous parcelles résultantes se superposent et alternent entre elles pour créer une mosaïque de pièces aux caractères, usages et espèces végétales différents. Le jardin dessiné, situé devant le salon, est un tapis de parterres alignés où alternent les espèces ornementales. Le potager est devant la cuisine et, enfin, la haie est un axe dans l'angle du jardin. La diversité est renforcée par l'évolutivité du jardin au fil de l'année.

Este jardín ha sido diseñado como lugar de recreo, como huerto y como prolongación del espacio habitable interior. Debido a su carácter lineal y sus pequeñas dimensiones, la opción de la subdivisión es una lógica solución de ordenación. La subparcelas resultantes se superponen y se alternan las unas a las otras creando un mosaico de piezas de diferentes caracteres, usos y especies vegetales. El jardín rayado, ubicado delante del salón, es un tapiz de parterres alineados en los que se alternan especies ornamentales. El huerto aparece delante de la cocina y, por último, un seto ejerce de rótula en la esquina del jardín. La diversidad viene reforzada por la variabilidad del jardín durante el año.

# The Passion Garden

### Design: Koselicka, urban- and landscape planners

Location: **Salzburg, Austria**

Construction date: **2002**

Photos: © **Koselicka**

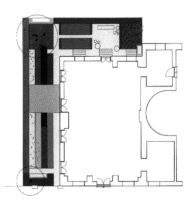

Elevation plan

■ The alchemist's garden is divided into two parts. The first is a botanical garden that collects varieties of plants used for popular magical ceremonies typical of Provence. The configuration of signs was conceived with the assistance of the ethnologist Pierre Lieutaghi. The second area represents a translation of the language of alchemy into an idiom proper to gardening. Special colors, forms, names and symbols abound in this garden, which is thought to have been the property of an alchemist in the 16th century. The two gardens complement each other in their recourse to symbolism.

■ Der Alchimistengarten ist in zwei Gärten gegliedert. Der erste ist eine Art botanischer Garten, in dem sich Pflanzenarten befinden, die bei provenzalischen Magierzeremonien verwendet wurden. Die Darstellung der Zeichen erfolgte unter Mitarbeit des Ethnologen Pierre Lieutaghi. Der zweite Garten stellt eine Übersetzung der alchimistischen Sprache in die der Gartenbaukunst dar. Farben, Formen, Namen und Symbole bevölkern diesen Garten, von dem angenommen wird, dass er Eigentum eines Alchimisten aus dem 16. Jahrhundert war. Die beiden Gärten ergänzen sich gegenseitig und spielen auf den Symbolismus an.

■ Le jardin de l'alchimiste est divisé en deux. Le premier espace est une manière de jardin botanique regroupant des espèces utilisées pour les cultes de magie populaire propres de la Provence. Le langage des signes a été conçu grâce à la collaboration de l'ethnologue Pierre Lieutaghi. Le second jardin représente une transposition du langage alchimique dans le langage propre au jardinage. Couleurs, formes, noms et symboles peuplent l'espace soupçonné d'appartenir à un alchimiste du XVIème siècle. Chaque jardin complète l'autre et invoque le symbolisme.

■ El jardín del alquimista es un jardín dividido en dos. El primero de ambos es una especie de jardín botánico que reagrupa especies utilizadas para ceremonias de magia popular propias de la Provence. El lenguaje de signos ha sido concebido gracias a la colaboración del etnólogo Pierre Lieutaghi. El segundo jardín representa una traducción del lenguaje alquímico al lenguaje propio de la jardinería. Colores, formas, nombres y símbolos pueblan este jardín que se sospecha que fue propiedad de un alquimista del siglo XVI. Ambos jardines se complementan y apelan al simbolismo.

# The Alchemist's Garden

### Design: Arnaud Maurières and Eric Ossart, gardeners

Location: **Eygalières, France**
Construction date: **1999**
Photos: **© Le Scanff-Mayer**

This store set out to create a design concept, going under the title "Humanature", that reflects the connection between human beings and their surroundings. To achieve this, the designers incorporated an element featuring vegetation. A long wall of plants behind a glass screen spans the length of the store, as well as extending up to the top floors. This installation contains more than 250 different plant species, including orchids, moss and ferns. The botanist Patrick Blanc has developed a technique that dispenses with soil; instead, a synthetic sheet soaked with water and fertilizer provides a base on which the plants can grow, turning this boutique into a living organism.

Unter dem Motto „Humanature" sollte diese Boutique so gestaltet werden, dass sie die Beziehung zwischen Menschen und ihrer Umgebung wiedergibt. Um dies zu erreichen haben die Designer Pflanzenelemente eingearbeitet. Eine große Pflanzenwand hinter einer Verglasung verläuft über die gesamte Höhe der Stockwerke des Geschäftes. Die Installation umfasst über 250 verschiedene Spezies, unter anderem Orchideen, Moose und Farne. Der Botaniker Patrick Blanc entwickelte eine Technik, mittels derer auf Bodensubstrat verzichtet werden kann. Eine mit Dünger und Wasser getränkte Synthetikleinwand dient als Grundlage für das Wachstum der Pflanzen. Die Boutique wird zu einem lebendigen Organismus.

Sous le lemme « Humanature », un concept de design a essayé d'être développé pour cette boutique, reflétant la connexion entre les humains et leur environnement. Pour ce, les créateurs incorporent l'élément végétal. Une grande paroi de plantes derrière une vitrine accompagne la boutique sur plusieurs niveaux. L'installation inclut plus de 250 espèces distinctes parmi lesquelles orchidées, mousses et fougères. Le botaniste Patrick Blanc a développé une technique permettant de se passer de sol. Une couverture synthétique mouillée d'eau et de fertilisants sert de base à la croissance des plantes. La boutique se transforme ainsi en un organisme vivant.

Bajo el lema "Humanature" se ha querido desarrollar un concepto de diseño que refleje la conexión entre los humanos y su entorno. Una gran pared de plantas tras una vitrina acompaña a esta tienda en los diferentes pisos. La instalación incluye más de 250 especies distintas entre las que se encuentran orquídeas, musgos y helechos. El botánico Patrick Blanc ha desarrollado una técnica que permite prescindir de tierra: una sábana sintética con agua y fertilizante sirve de base para el crecimiento de las plantas, de manera que la boutique se convierte en un organismo vivo.

# Girbaud's Vertical Garden
**Design: Kristian Gavoille, architect, and Patrick Blanc, botanist**

Location: **Paris, France**
Construction date: **2002**
Photos: © **Mihail Moldoveanu**

The space devoted to the garden of the Pershing Hall Hotel is basically a small rectangle between the high facades of the surrounding buildings. As it is enclosed in this way, it receives virtually no direct sunlight, and in summertime the restaurant's tables occupy practically all the usable ground space. These two factors would seem to rule out the presence of any vegetation, but Putman and Blanck came up with the solution of exploiting one of the walls to create a vertical garden, mainly consisting of climbing plants. This "two-dimensional" garden stretches up to the top of the hotel and can be seen from all its floors.

Der Garten des Hotels Pershing Hall ist im Grunde ein kleines Rechteck zwischen den hochragenden Fassaden und Brandmauern der angrenzenden Grundstücke. Aufgrund der ihn umgebenden Bebauung ist nahezu kein direkter Lichteinfall vorhanden, und während des Sommers nehmen die Tische des Restaurants fast die gesamte Nutzfläche ein. Angesichts dieser scheinbar mit einer Bepflanzung unvereinbaren Situation bestand die Lösung von Putman und Blanck in einem an eine der Mauern angelehnten vertikalen, hauptsächlich aus Kletterpflanzen bestehenden Garten. Dieser „zweidimensionale Garten" verläuft längs der gesamten Höhe des Hotels und ist von den verschiedenen Stockwerken aus zu sehen.

L'espace destiné au jardin de l'hôtel Pershing Hall est, en fin de compte, un petit rectangle entre de hautes façades les partitions des parcelles voisines. En raison de la fermeture subie, l'entrée directe de la lumière solaire est presque inexistante. Durant l'été, les tables de restaurant occupent pratiquement toute la superficie utile. Étant donnée la situation apparemment incompatible avec la présence d'éléments végétaux, Putman et Blanck ont proposé de s'appuyer sur l'un des murs pour développer un jardin à la verticale, formée essentiellement de plantes grimpantes. Ce jardin en « deux dimensions » accompagne l'hôtel en hauteur et demeure visible depuis chaque étage.

El espacio destinado al jardín del hotel de Pershing Hall es, en resumidas cuentas, un pequeño rectángulo entre altas fachadas y medianeras de las parcelas colindantes. Debido al cerramiento al que se encuentra sometido, la entrada directa de la luz solar es casi inexistente. Durante el verano, las mesas del restaurante ocupan prácticamente toda la superficie útil. Dada la situación aparentemente incompatible con la presencia de elementos vegetales, la solución propuesta por Putman y Blanck ha sido apoyarse sobre uno de los muros para desarrollar un jardín en vertical, formado principalmente por plantas trepadoras. Este jardín "de dos dimensiones" acompaña al hotel en altura y queda visible desde las diferentes plantas.

# Garden of Pershing Hall

### Design: Andrée Putman, architect, and Patrick Blanck, botanist

Location: **Paris, France**
Construction date: **2001**
Photos: **© Mihail Moldoveanu**

▓ This small garden is characterized by the use of a theatrical language typical of this designer, in keeping with the rest of the project. Its position next to the main room of the restaurant makes it an important focal point as it provides a source of sunlight. There are strong visual links between these two spaces, and the elements that form the garden acquire the dramatic impact of theater scenery. A long stone wall props up large steel tubs containing miniature, vertical gardens made up of beds of ivy. These "living canvases" emphasize the importance of this garden's contemplative aspects, as well as illustrating the concept of a garden as an exhibition.

▓ Dieser kleine Garten ist durch die eigenwillige theatrale Ausdrucksform seines Gestalters gekennzeichnet, die sich über das gesamte Projekt erstreckt. Er bildet die Fortsetzung des Hauptsaales des Restaurants und wird so zu einer Tageslichtquelle. Hierdurch und auch aufgrund der starken visuellen Verbindung zwischen diesen beiden Räumen erhalten die strukturbildenden Komponenten des Gartens nahezu bühnenbildnerische Bedeutung. Längs der vorhandenen Steinmauer sind großformatige Stahlrahmen angelehnt, in denen sich senkrechte Gartenausschnitte aus Efeu befinden. Diese „lebenden Leinwände" heben die Bedeutung der kontemplativen Funktion dieses Gartens und das Konzepts eines ausgestellten Gartens hervor.

▓ Ce petit jardin est caractérisé par l'emploi d'un langage théâtral propre au créateur et commun au reste du projet. Sa situation à la suite de la salle principale du restaurant le convertit en un foyer important d'entrée de lumière. De ce fait, et de par la forte connexion visuelle existante entre ces deux espace, les éléments structurant le jardin affichent une importance quasi scénographique. Le long du mur de pierre existant s'appuient des cadres d'acier aux grandes dimensions qui couvrent en leur intérieur des parties de jardins verticaux, formés par le lierre. Ces « toiles vivantes » soulignent l'importance de la fusion contemplative de ce jardin et du concept du jardin exposé.

▓ Este pequeño jardín se caracteriza por el empleo de un lenguaje teatral muy propio del diseñador y común al resto del proyecto. Su ubicación a continuación de la sala principal del restaurante lo convierte en un importante foco de entrada de luz. Los elementos que estructuran el jardín reciben una importancia casi escenográfica. A lo largo del muro piedra se apoyan unos marcos de acero de grandes dimensiones que abarcan en su interior recortes de jardines en vertical formados por hiedras. Estos "lienzos vivos" remarcan la importancia de la función contemplativa de este jardín y el concepto del jardín expuesto.

# Garden in Bon
### Design: Philippe Stark, designer

Location: **Paris, France**

Construction date: **2000**

Photos: © **Mihail Moldoveanu**

317

■ In a restricted space the planning of a garden can easily move from the horizontal plane to the vertical one. The main structure in this garden is a screen made of highly permeable industrial fabric, with pouches sewn on to it. Discreet streams of water trickling down the material and the addition of fertile soil to the pouches have encouraged the growth of an abundance of plants normally found only in humid environments. This vertical, almost two-dimensional element adds an enormous visual interest to this small garden, inviting comparisons with a painting—but one that paints itself.

■ In einem Raum von begrenzten Ausmaßen ist bei der Gartengestaltung der Übergang von der waagrechten in die senkrechte Ebene ein Leichtes. Die tragende Struktur dieses Gartens ist eine sehr durchlässige Bespannung aus Industriegewebe mit aufgenähten Taschen. Ein dünner, über das Gewebe gleitender Wasserfilm und Pflanzensubstrat in den Taschen ermöglichen das Gedeihen einer großen Vielfalt von Pflanzenarten aus Feuchtgebieten. Die vertikale, beinahe zweidimensionale Komponente erhält eine starke bildnerische Ausdruckskraft innerhalb des kleinen Gartens und kann als Leinwand verstanden werden, die sich selbst bemalt.

■ Dans un espace aux dimensions réduites, la concrétisation d'un jardin passe facilement du plan horizontal au plan vertical. Un écran de tissu industriel très perméable, avec des bourses cousues, est la structure principale de ce jardin. Une vague d'eau qui descend sur la toile et la présence de substrat fertile dans les poches permettent la prolifération d'une diversité d'espèces végétales propres des zones humides. Cet élément vertical, presque bidimensionnel, prend une grande force picturale dans ce petit jardin, qui peut être lu comme une toile qui se dessinerait d'elle-même.

■ En un espacio de dimensiones reducidas la concretización de un jardín pasa con facilidad del plano horizontal al vertical. Una pantalla de tejido industrial de gran permeabilidad, con bolsillos cosidos a ella, es la estructura principal de este jardín. Una sutil lámina de agua que desciende por la tela y la presencia de sustrato fértil en los bolsillos permiten la proliferación de una gran diversidad de especies vegetales propias de ambientes húmedos. Este elemento vertical, casi bidimensional, adquiere un gran fuerza pintoresca dentro del pequeño jardín que puede ser leído como un lienzo que va dibujándose a sí mismo.

# Film-maker's Garden

**Design: Terragram Pty. Ltd., landscape architects**

Location: **Sydney, Australia**
Construction date: **1998**
Photos: © **Terragram Pty. Ltd.**

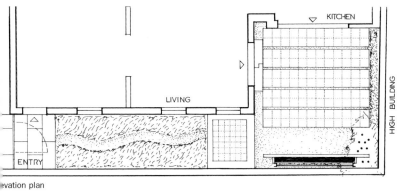

...vation plan

The house was built to follow the craggy terrain and the pre-existing vegetation has been preserved as much as possible. The pine tree protrudes through the pergola, built on the main part of the plot—also occupied by the house—and provides shade, which is intensified in summer by a climbing vine. The vegetation is rounded off by other species growing on the walls, as well as the more domestic flowers that fill the gaps between the shrubs that have spilled over from the nearby wood. Perhaps the most noticeable feature of this garden is the smooth transition between the intimate and private space of the house and the exuberance of the natural world beyond.

Das Haus ist auf einem stark abschüssigen Gelände gebaut und es wurde versucht die Bepflanzung weitestmöglich zu erhalten. Durch die Pinie wird die Wirkung der Pergola auf dem Grundstück durchbrochen. Der Schatten, den sie im Sommer spendet, wird durch Weinlaub verstärkt. Hinzu kommen andere Pflanzenspezies an den Mauern und einheimische Gewächse, welche die Lücken zwischen den Büschen und Sträuchern aus dem angrenzenden Wald auffüllen. Der einprägsamste Eindruck dieses Gartens ist vielleicht der sanfte Übergang zwischen dem zurückgezogenen Raum um das Haus und der üppigen Vegetation der unmittelbaren Umgebung.

La demeure, située sur un terrain urbain limitrophe de la sierra de Collserolla, s'organise autour de gradins de pierre Llicorella afin de s'adapter aux forts dénivelés du site. Sur la terrasse principale, pavée de dalles formant un carroyage, se dresse une pergola qui voit grimper une vigne. La végétation existante sur le site a été intégrée dans le projet de maison. Un exemple en est le pin pignon (Pinus pinea) qui interrompt la pergola. La sensation la plus perceptible de ce jardin repose dans la douce transition entre l'intime et privé ceignant la maison, en continuité avec la nature exubérante si proche.

La casa se construyó a partir de la fuerte preexistencia del terreno escarpado intentando salvar al máximo la vegetación. El pino interrumpe la pérgola, que se desarrolla en el bancal principal que ocupa la casa, proporcionando una sombra que se completa en verano con una parra. Se ha completado la vegetación con otras especies que pueblan los muros y flores más domésticas que rellenan los huecos entre arbustos propios del bosque vecino. Quizás la sensación más perceptible de este jardín es la suave transición entre el mundo íntimo y privado alrededor de la casa en continuidad con la exuberante naturaleza próxima.

# Pla House
### Design: Various architects

Location: **Barcelona, Spain**

Construction date: **1987**

Photos: © **Mihail Moldoveanu**

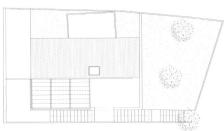

Elevation plan

0 5

The gardens of the Federal Railroad Department ("Eisenbahnbundesamt") aim for a conceptual approximation of the dynamics of linear elements, starting from the railroad track that marks the boundaries of the grounds. A garden based around a number of shrubs has been created, with a wooden walkway linking the building and the railroad tracks. This garden, almost thematic in nature, sets up an interplay of shadows and movement. The shadows seem to be etched onto the flooring, while pedestrians pass between the main building and the station by crossing the area that is studded with trees.

Der Garten des Eisenbahnbundesamts setzt auf eine konzeptuelle Annäherung an die Dynamik linearer Elemente. Ausgehend von der das Grundstück begrenzenden Eisenbahnlinie entwickelt sich ein Garten mit Büschen und einem Holzweg, der zwischen dem Gebäude und den Schienen verläuft. Dieser Garten, der stark an einen Themenpark erinnert lebt von dem Spiel aus Schatten und Bewegung. Die Schatten erscheinen wie ins Pflaster eingraviert während sich die Benutzer zwischen dem Hauptgebäude und dem Bahnhof durch den baumbestandenen Bereich bewegen.

Le jardin du Service fédéral des chemins de fer (« Eisenbahnbundesamt ») parie sur une approche conceptuelle de la dynamique des éléments linéaires. Partant de la ligne de chemin de fer délimitant la parcelle du projet, un jardin d'arbustes est développé entre l'édifice et les voies ferrées, parcouru par un chemin de planches. Ce jardin au caractère quasi thématique propose un jeu d'ombres et de mouvement. Les ombres apparaissent comme gravées sur le sol alors que les usagers circulent de l'édifice principal à la station en traversant la partie boisée.

El jardín del Departamento Federal de Ferrocarriles ("Eisenbahnbundesamt") apuesta por un aproximación conceptual a la dinámica de los elementos lineales. Partiendo de la línea de ferrocarril que delimita la parcela de actuación se desarrolla un jardín de setos con un camino de madera que lo recorre entre la edificación y las vías de tren. Este jardín, de carácter casi temático, propone un juego de sombras y movimiento. Las sombras aparecen grabadas sobre el pavimento, mientras que los usuarios circulan entre el edificio principal y la estación atravesando la zona arbolada.

# Eisenbahnbundesamt

Design: TOPOTEK 1, landscape architects

Location: **Berlin, Germany**
Construction date: **2001**
Photos: © **Hanns Joosten**

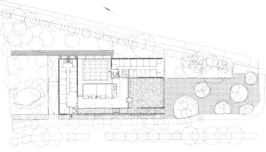

Elevation plan

■ This project for a garden on the terrace of a residential block in the heart of Vienna is divided into three areas that are differentiated from each other according to the uses for which they are intended. The so-called "Hortus conclusus" is an intimate, shut-off space dominated by plants and natural stone. The second area, which serves as a belvedere, uses materials that evoke the deck of a boat: wood, glass and metal. Finally, the largest area is planted with several varieties of hardy and strikingly colored plants. A series of gravel paths meander through these plants to create an arresting visual pattern.

■ Dieses Gartenprojekt auf der Dachterrasse eines Wohngebäudes im Herzen Wiens umfasst drei nach ihrer Verwendung unterschiedliche Bereiche. Im sogenannten „Hortus conclusus", einem abgeschlossenen und in sich selbst zurückgezogenen Ort, herrschen pflanzliche Elemente und Naturstein vor. Im zweiten Bereich, der als Aussichtspunkt dient, spielen die verwendeten Materialarten auf ein Schiffsdeck an: Holz, Glas und Metall. Der größte Bereich schließlich ist mit verschiedenen Arten leuchtend farbiger Dickblattgewächse bepflanzt. Ein Kiesweg verläuft durch die Pflanzung und erzeugt einen an Graphikdesign erinnernden Eindruck.

■ Ce projet de jardin, sur le toit en terrasse d'un immeuble de logements au cœur de Vienne, intègre trois espaces différenciés selon l'usage auquel ils sont destinés. Le dénommé « Hortus conclusus » est un lieu intime et clos sur lui même où prédomine l'élément végétal et la pierre naturelle. Dans le deuxième espace, s'offrant en point de vue, les matériaux employés font allusion à un pont de bateau : bois, verre et métal. Enfin, l'espace le plus vaste est occupé par une plantation de diverses espèces de plantes grasses aux couleurs très vives. Un sentier en gravier traverse la plantation et génère une image proche de celle du design graphique.

■ Este proyecto de jardín en el terrado de un edificio de viviendas en el corazón de Viena incorpora tres espacios diferenciados según los usos a los que se destinan. El denominado "Hortus conclusus" es un lugar íntimo y cerrado en sí mismo en el que predomina el elemento vegetal y la piedra natural. En el segundo espacio, que ejerce de mirador, los materiales empleados hacen alusión a una cubierta de barco: madera, cristal y metal. Por último, el espacio de mayores dimensiones está ocupado por una plantación de distintas especies de plantas grasas de fuerte cromatismo. Un camino de grava atraviesa la plantación y genera una imagen cercana al diseño gráfico.

# Terrace Garden in Vienna

**Design: 3:0 Landschaftsarchitektur, Gachowetz, Lutz, Zimmermann, landscape architects**

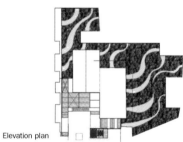

Elevation plan

Location: **Vienna, Austria**

Construction date: **2002**

Photos: © **3:0 Landschaftsarchitektur**

Perspective drawing

▨ The Marianne Boesky garden is situated in a terrace in downtown Manhattan flanked to the east, west and south by buildings that block out the sunlight. The vegetation has been chosen with this inconvenience in mind. Lines of large tiles mark out a grid, with eight squares covered exactly by a wooden tub, each containing a specimen of *Betula nigra*. The northern side has been exploited as the site for a summerhouse. This construction, designed by Richard Gluckman, aims to create a focal point, inviting the garden's users to enjoy its comforts, once they have passed the set of fir trees, carefully arranged to give the impression of a miniature city park.

▨ Der Garten von Marianne Boesky befindet sich auf einer Terrasse im unteren Teil von Manhattan und ist im Osten, Westen und Süden von Gebäuden umgeben, die keine direkte Lichteinwirkung zulassen. Dieser Umstand war Ausgangspunkt bei der Wahl der Bepflanzung. Ein schachbrettartiger Plattenbelag dient als Rahmen für die Bepflanzung mit *Betula nigra* in acht Holzkübeln. Für die Errichtung eines Pavillons wurde die Nordseite gewählt. Nach einem Design von Richard Gluckman soll mit diesem ein Schwerpunkt geschaffen werden, auf den man nach Durchqueren einer kleinen Birkenpflanzung wie durch einen kleinen, persönlichen Stadtpark zustrebt.

▨ Le jardin de Marianne Boesky se trouve sur une terrasse du bas de Manhattan, entourée à l'ouest, à l'est et au sud d'immeubles lui interdisant l'accès direct à la lumière. La végétation sélectionnée part de cette prémisse. Une grille de pavage en carreaux sert de cadre de plantation pour situer les huit conteneurs en bois avec leurs exemplaires respectifs de *Betula nigra*. La face nord a été choisie pour y construire un pavillon. L'emplacement de cette pièce, conçue par Richard Gluckman, prétend créer un point focal vers lequel se diriger, non sans traverser auparavant la petite plantation de bouleaux, comme on le ferait d'un petit parc citadin personnel.

▨ El jardín de Marianne Boesky se encuentra ubicado en una terraza del bajo Manhattan circundada a los lados este, oeste y sur por edificios que impiden la entrada de luz directa. La vegetación escogida parte de esta premisa. Una cuadrícula de pavimento de baldosas sirve de marco de plantación para ubicar los ocho contenedores de madera con sus respectivos ejemplares de *Betula nigra*. El lado norte ha sido escogido como lugar para construir un pabellón. La ubicación de esta pieza, diseñada por Richard Gluckman, pretende crear un punto focal al que dirigirse, no sin antes atravesar la pequeña plantación de abedules como quien atraviesa un pequeño y personal parque urbano.

# Marianne Boesky Garden
### Design: Paula Hayes, landscape designer

Location: **New York, USA**
Construction date: **2000**
Photos: **© John Peden**

■ The garden area typical of the arid Mediterranean setting that can also be used as an open-air projection suite. Metal structures were placed around the pre-existing lights to form climbing frames for plants and a support for the benches. The paving is made of several types of sandstone of varying textures, and the access areas have been reinforced by grills made of galvanized steel. The vegetation includes aromatic shrubs, cacti and climbing plants, all requiring minimum upkeep. The ramps will be covered with creepers, while the higher ramps at the ends of the patio will combine with climbing plants to partially enclose the space.

■ Der Gartenbereich mit trockenem, mediterranem Charakter soll als Freiluftkino dienen. Metallstrukturen um die vorhandenen Lichtschächte begrenzen die bepflanzten Böschungen und werden zu Bänken. Der Bodenbelag besteht aus grobem Sand von unterschiedlicher Korngröße mit variablem Anteil an organischer Materie. Die Durchgangsbereiche sind durch Gitter aus verzinktem Stahl verstärkt. Die Bepflanzung besteht aus buschbildenden aromatischen Pflanzen, Dickblattgewächsen und Kletterpflanzen, die wenig Pflege erfordern. Die Böschungen werden langsam von Bodendeckern bewachsen, während den Innenhof höhere Böschungen und Kletterpflanzen teilweise umschließen.

■ La zone paysagère au caractère sec et méditerranéen s'utilisent comme salle de projection à l'air libre. La disposition de structures métalliques autour des lucernaires existants forme les plans inclinés des plantations et le soutien des bancs. Le revêtement sablonneux offre différentes granulométries avec plus ou moins de matière organique. Les zones de passage sont renforcées à l'aide de grilles d'acier galvanisé. La végétation comprend des plantes aromatiques en buisson, des plantes grasses et grimpantes, chacune avec des besoins d'entretien minimes. Les talus finiront par être couverts de plantes rampantes, alors qu'aux limites du patio, des talus plus hauts et des plantes grimpantes génèrent une fermeture partielle.

■ La zona ajardinada de carácter seco mediterráneo se utiliza como sala de proyecciones al aire libre. Unas estructuras metálicas alrededor de los lucernarios existentes forman los taludes de plantación y el soporte para los bancos. La pavimentación es de sablón de diferentes granulometrías con más o menos materia orgánica. Las zonas de paso se refuerzan mediante rejas de acero galvanizado. La vegetación incluye plantas arbustivas aromáticas, plantas grasas y plantas trepadoras, todas ellas con unas exigencias de mantenimiento mínimas. Los taludes acabarán recubriéndose de tapizantes, mientras que en los límites del patio, taludes de mayor altura y plantas trepadoras provocarán un cerramiento parcial.

# Patio Zindara

**Design: Edda Manrique, sculptor, and Raimon Corberó, gardener**

Location: **Barcelona, Spain**
Construction date: **2002**
Photos: **© Alejandro Bahamón**

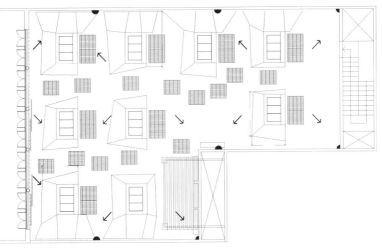

Elevation plan

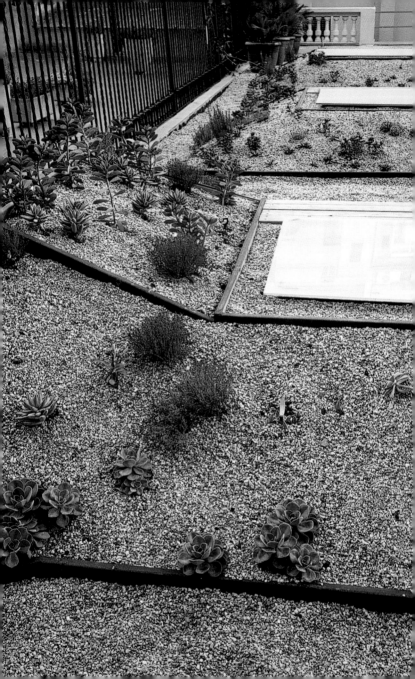

■ The main emphasis of this garden is the use of contemporary materials, rather than any radical spatial configurations. The L-shape plot is articulated around an apple tree. The garden is organized in a series of terraces bounded by beams treated with aluminum which provide support for galvanized steel grilles. An aluminum duct allows water to pass down the tiers of the terraces. Two edges of the garden are defined by the presence of bamboo, the third by an aluminum screen. Another aluminum screen also separates the roof terrace from the neighbors, while two illuminated acrylic cylinders give this space its special character.

■ Dieser Garten zeichnet sich besonders durch die Ablehnung der Suche nach einem narrativen Inhalt zugunsten der Verwendung zeitgemäßer Materialien aus. Das L-förmige Grundstück erstreckt sich um einen Apfelbaum. Vertikal ist der Garten in Terrassen unterteilt, die von Aluminiumbalken eingefasst sind, auf denen Gitter aus verzinktem Stahl liegen. In einem stufenförmig die Terrassen durchlaufenden Aluminiumkanal fließt Wasser. An zwei Seiten ist der Garten durch Bambus begrenzt und an der dritten durch eine Aluminiumabschirmung. Auf der Terrasse dient eine weitere Aluminiumwand als Einrahmung für die Galerie. Zwei beleuchtete Acrylzylinder verleihen dem Ort seine Atmosphäre.

■ Le refus de la quête d'un contenu narratif pour utiliser des matériaux contemporains est la principale caractéristique de ce jardin. La parcelle en forme de L s'articule autour d'un pommier. En hauteur, le jardin s'organise en terrasses contenues par des poutres métallisées à l'aluminium, sur lesquelles s'appuient des grilles d'acier galvanisé. Un canal d'aluminium que l'eau parcourre suit la forme échelonnée des terrasses. Deux des limites du jardin sont définies par la présence de bambou ; la troisième par une cloison d'aluminium. Depuis la terrasse, un autre panneau d'aluminium sert de cadre pour le mirador. Deux cylindres éclairés en acrylique singularisent l'atmosphère de l'espace.

■ El rechazo de la búsqueda de un contenido narrativo a favor de la utilización de materiales contemporáneos es la principal característica de este jardín. La parcela en forma de L se articula entorno a un manzano. En altura, el jardín se organiza en terrazas contenidas por vigas metalizadas con aluminio, sobre las que se apoyan rejillas de acero galvanizado. Un canal de aluminio por el que transcurre agua recorre de forma escalonada las terrazas. Dos de los límites del jardín se definen por la presencia de bambú; el tercero, por una pantalla de aluminio. Desde la terraza otra pantalla de aluminio ejerce de marco para el mirador. Dos cilindros iluminados de acrílico ambientan el espacio.

# Aluminium Garden
### Design: Ken Smith, landscape architect

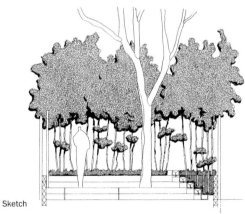

Sketch

Location: **New York, USA**

Construction date: **1999**

Photos: **© Betsy Pinover Schiff / Ken Smith**

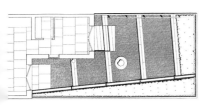

Elevation plan

■ The rectangular form of the terrace and the house in the center of the plot reduce the usable gardening space to two longitudinal strips and two small spaces at the ends. The area with the most sunlight contains the swimming pool, which is clad with pieces of pottery that form a pattern. The flooring on the terrace is made of iroko wood. The generous dimensions of the wooden tubs on the two long strips of garden allow both the Mediterranean vegetation (*Pittosporum, Myoporum, Lagestroemia and Photinia*) to isolate the garden and the climbing plants (*Wisteria sinensis, Rosa banksiae and Ampelopsis*) to almost completely cover the metal structure of the pergola.

■ Die rechteckige Form der Terrasse und das Wohnhaus im Zentrum reduzieren die Nutzfläche des Gartens auf zwei längliche Streifen und zwei kleine Räume an den Enden. Dort wo die Sonneneinstahlung am stärksten ist, befindet sich der Swimmingpool, der mit Keramikstücken im Damaszenermuster verkleidet ist. Der Bodenbelag der Terrasse besteht aus Iroko-Holz. Die großen Pflanzenkübel an den Längsseiten des Gartens gestatten einerseits seine Abschirmung durch mediterrane Vegetation (*Pittosporum, Myoporum, Lagestroemia und Photinia*) und andererseits, dass die Kletterpflanzen (*Wisteria sinensis, Rosa banksiae und Ampelopsis*) die Metallstruktur der Pergola fast ganz bedecken.

■ La forme rectangulaire de la terrasse et la présence centrale de la maison réduisent l'espace utile du jardin à deux franges longitudinales et à deux espaces aux extrémités. Revêtue de pièces de céramique formant un damas, la piscine se situe dans la zone la plus ensoleillée. Le sol de la terrasse est recouvert de bois d'iroko. Les grandes dimensions des jardinières de bois situées dans les deux franges longitudinales du jardin permettent, d'un côté, que la végétation méditerranéenne (*Pittosporum, Myoporum, Lagestroemia et Photinia*) isole le jardin et que, d'un autre côté, des plantes grimpantes (*Wisteria sinensis, Rosa banksiae et Ampelopsis*) couvrent presque complètement la pergola au profil métallique.

■ La forma rectangular de la terraza y la presencia central de la vivienda reducen el espacio útil del jardín a dos franjas longitudinales y dos pequeños espacios en los extremos. En la zona de máximo sol se ubica la piscina, revestida de piezas de cerámica formando adamascado. El pavimento de la terraza es de madera de iroko. Las grandes dimensiones de las jardineras de madera ubicadas en las dos franjas longitudinales del jardín permiten, por un lado, que la vegetación mediterránea (*Pittosporum, Myoporum, Lagestroemia y Photinia*) aísle el jardín y, por el otro, que plantas trepadoras (*Wisteria sinensis, Rosa banksiae y Ampelopsis*) cubran casi por completo la pérgola de perfilería metálica.

# Private Roofgarden

### Design: Pepe Cortés, designer

Location: **Barcelona, Spain**

Construction date: **1998**

Photos: © **Alejandro Bahamón**

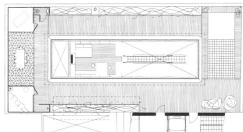

Elevation plan 1

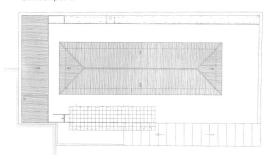

Elevation plan 2

■ This project formed part of a wider planification encompassing the restoration of an old distillery. Outdoors, the designers' intervention prolonged the interior space with two large terraces left open to the fury of the wind. Although the two areas are separate, the whole is unified by the strong presence of bamboo as the main vegetal element. The meticulous attention to detail and the array of different materials (steel girders, canopies made of cloth, stainless-steel edges, wooden planks, untreated paving stones, mobile plant tubs and pools of water) draw the eye to the individual elements in these spaces designed for individual and collective use.

■ Das Projekt ist Teil eines umfassenden Plans für die Instandsetzung einer ehemaligen Destillerie. Der Außenbereich ist in zwei große, heftigen Winden ausgesetzte Terrassen unterteilt, die als Verlängerung des Innenraums konzipiert wurden und trotz ihres unterschiedlichen Charakters durch die vorherrschende Präsenz von Bambus als tragendem Element der Bepflanzung miteinander verbunden sind. Die sorgfältige Gestaltung der Fläche und die technischen Details (Stahlträger, Schattenspender aus Stoff, Rahmen aus rostfreiem Stahl, Bodenbeläge aus Holz und Naturstein, bewegliche Pflanzenkübel und Teiche) unterstreichen die Auflösung und Bewertung der verschiedenen räumlichen Unterteilungen für gemeinschaftliche und individuelle Nutzung.

■ Le projet s'insère dans un plan global de restauration d'une ancienne distillerie. L'intervention sur les extérieurs se divise en deux grandes terrasses exposées à de forts vents. Les deux espaces pensés comme une prolongation de l'espace interne sont des lieux distincts mais unis par la forte présence du bambou, l'élément végétal principal. Le design méticuleux de la superficie et les détails techniques (poutres d'acier, tonnelle en toile, cadres d'acier inoxydable, revêtement de bois et de pierre naturelle, conteneurs de plantes mobiles et réservoirs d'eau) provoquent la décomposition et la valorisation des diverses pièces de ces espaces, destinés à un usage collectif et individuel.

■ El proyecto se insiere en un proyecto global de restauración de una antigua destilería. La intervención de los exteriores se divide en dos grandes terrazas expuestas a fuertes vientos. Los dos espacios concebidos como prolongación del espacio interno son lugares distintos pero unidos por la fuerte presencia del bambú como elemento vegetal principal. El diseño meticuloso de la superficie y los detalles técnicos (vigas de acero, umbráculos de tela, marcos de acero inoxidable, pavimentos de madera y piedra natural, contenedores móviles de plantas y balsas de agua) provocan la descomposición y valoración de las distintas piezas de estos espacios destinados al uso colectivo e individual.

# Roofgarden in Venice

**Design: Daniela Moderini, Laura Zampieri and Ippolito Pizetti, architects**

Location: **Venice, Italy**
Construction date: **1999**
Photos: © **Moderini / Zampieri**

Sketches

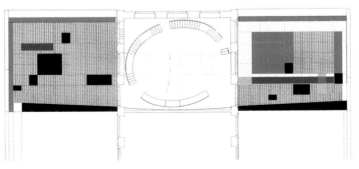

Elevation plan

◼ The setting for this garden is a terrace in Manhattan. Its exposure to strong west winds and intense sunlight has determined the choice of plants. Hedges of *Juniperus*, *Taxus* and *Forsythias* and clumps of evergreens add rural touches to the rigorously geometric layout of the plant tubs, intended to reflect the urban sprawl down below, with its alternating constructions and demolitions. The presence of the city is inescapable, as it is continually glimpsed through the various visual openings. The only respite is found in the two intimate spaces of the cedar-wood pergola and the interior of the apartment.

◼ Der Garten befindet sich auf einer Terrasse in Manhattan. Bei der Auswahl der Pflanzenarten wurden der heftige Westwind sowie die starke Sonneneinstrahlung berücksichtigt. Hecken von *Juniperus* und *Taxus*, *Forsythias* und dichte Blumenbeete aus immergrünen Pflanzen verleihen der streng geometrischen Anordnung der Kübel einen ländlichen Charakter. Das der Anordnung zugrunde liegende Raster bezieht sich auf die urbane Landschaft, in der sich sowohl im Bau als auch im Abriss befindliche Grundstücke abwechseln. Die Stadt bleibt durch die verschiedenen Durchblicke stets präsent. Die Pergola aus Zedernholz und das Innere der Wohnung sind die einzigen geschützten Räume.

◼ Le jardin se situe sur une terrasse de Manhattan. Les forts vents d'ouest et la surexposition solaire conditionnent le choix des espèces végétales. Haies de *Juniperus* et de *Taxus*, *Forsythias* et massifs de pérennes apportent une touche rurale à un ordonnancement de conteneurs strictement géométrique. La trame à partir de laquelle s'organise la végétation fait référence au paysage urbain où alternent constructions et démolitions. La ville se fait présente depuis les différentes ouvertures visuelles. La pergola en bois de cèdre et l'intérieur de la demeure restent les seuls espaces d'intimité.

◼El jardín se encuentra ubicado en una terraza de Manhattan. Los fuertes vientos del oeste, así como la fuerte exposición solar, condicionan la elección de las especies vegetales. Setos de *Juniperus* y *Taxus*, *Forsythias* y macizos de perennes aportan el carácter rural a una ordenación de contenedores estrictamente geométrica. La trama a partir de la cual se organiza la vegetación hace referencia al paisaje urbano en el que se alternan construcciones y demoliciones. La ciudad se hace presente a partir de las diferentes aperturas visuales. La pérgola de madera de cedro y el interior de la vivienda restan como los únicos espacios de intimidad.

# Chris & Illya Vroom Garden

### Design: Paula Hayes, landscape designer

Location: **New York, USA**
Construction date: **2000**
Photos: © **John Peden**

Elevation plan

**Other Designpocket titles by teNeues:**

**Asian Interior Design** 3-8238-4527-6

**Bathroom Design** 3-8238-4523-3

**Berlin Apartments** 3-8238-5596-4

**Cafés & Restaurants** 3-8238-5478-X

**Cool Hotels** 3-8238-5556-5

**Country Hotels** 3-8238-5574-3

**Exhibition Design** 3-8238-5548-4

**Furniture/Möbel/Meubles/Mobile Design** 3-8238-5575-1

**Italian Interior Design** 3-8238-5495-X

**Kitchen Design** 3-8238-4522-5

**London Apartments** 3-8238-5558-1

**Los Angeles Houses** 3-8238-5594-8

**New York Apartments** 3-8238-5557-3

**Office Design** 3-8238-5578-6

**Paris Apartments** 3-8238-5571-9

**Product Design** 3-8238-5597-2

**San Francisco Houses** 3-8238-4526-8

**Showrooms** 3-8238-5496-8

**Spa & Wellness Hotels** 3-8238-5595-6

**Staircases** 3-8238-5572-7

**Sydney Houses** 3-8238-4525-x

**Tokyo Houses** 3-8238-5573-5

Each volume:

12.5 x 18.5 cm
400 pages
c. 400 color illustrations